A Long Way from Whitehall

A Long Way from Whitehall

DAVID LYNN LYONS

Copyright © 2014 David Lynn Lyons.

All rights reserved. No part of this book may be used or reproduced by any means, graphic, electronic, or mechanical, including photocopying, recording, taping or by any information storage retrieval system without the written permission of the publisher except in the case of brief quotations embodied in critical articles and reviews.

Archway Publishing books may be ordered through booksellers or by contacting:

Archway Publishing
1663 Liberty Drive
Bloomington, IN 47403
www.archwaypublishing.com
1-(888)-242-5904

Because of the dynamic nature of the Internet, any web addresses or links contained in this book may have changed since publication and may no longer be valid. The views expressed in this work are solely those of the author and do not necessarily reflect the views of the publisher, and the publisher hereby disclaims any responsibility for them.

Any people depicted in stock imagery provided by Thinkstock are models, and such images are being used for illustrative purposes only. Certain stock imagery © Thinkstock.

ISBN: 978-1-4808-0950-5 (sc)
ISBN: 978-1-4808-0952-9 (hc)
ISBN: 978-1-4808-0951-2 (e)

Library of Congress Control Number: 2014913489

Printed in the United States of America.

Archway Publishing rev. date: 10/9/2014

This book is dedicated to my devoted wife Cathy who encouraged me to write my story and who stood by me throughout the process. She always provided valuable input and counsel as she patiently read each new chapter. She alternated between uncontrolled laughter and shaking her head, all the while saying "I don't know if you should tell that." In the end she always reached the same conclusion, which was, this is your story, tell it your way. I also want to dedicate it to my first wife and mother of my son. Bernice was an integral part of most of the story and lived it with me. She always supported any crazy idea that I had and lived through some tough times with me. The most important thing that she did was give me the best son that a father could ever hope for and for that I am eternally grateful.

INTRODUCTION

> "To every man there comes that special moment when he is tapped on the shoulder and offered a chance to do a very special thing unique unto him. What a tragedy if that moment finds him unprepared for that which would be his finest hour."

These words, spoken by Sir Winston Churchill during his tenure as prime minister of Great Britain, make up my favorite quote of all time. The quote also somewhat sums up my life and is one of the primary reasons I wrote this book.

A Long Way from Whitehall is my story. It is a story of a poor country kid who the world said had no chance of ever making anything of himself and who, in spite of the odds, found a way to succeed. It is a story of ups and downs, adventures and misadventures. Some of the story is funny. Some of it is hard to read without crying. It is all true.

I chose to write the book because I wanted to leave something for my grandchildren. I wanted them to know something about a lifestyle that is now gone forever. I don't believe that even in the remote mountains of Appalachia, there are folks who live today as I did growing up.

I have told the story here as I remember it. I have included the good along with the bad, and many of the things I have written about are not my proudest moments. I do believe, however, that all of the experiences reflected in this book have made me a better person and ensured when that special moment came, I was indeed prepared.

This is a story about a boy who overcame a life of poverty to become an "officer and a gentleman" as a commissioned officer in the US Army.

Now there are thousands of young men and women commissioned every year in the armed services. That in itself is not worthy of writing a book. However, my story is more than that. The fact I became a commissioned officer in spite of my upbringing and with all the odds stacked against me is the real story. When I left home at seventeen to join the navy, no one would have thought in a million years that I would ever amount to anything. Certainly, no one would have believed I would have a successful career in not only the military but in law enforcement.

The book ends at my commissioning ceremony, but the truth is, my life began on that day. Being a commissioned officer is more than wearing bars and getting salutes from subordinates. It is about honor and always doing the right thing. It is about taking care of your troops and putting them first, even at great sacrifice to yourself. The words "duty, honor, country" actually mean something. It means you would willfully lay down your life for your fellow service member without hesitation. Every day I tried to uphold the oath I took with every task.

I completed a career of over twenty years and retired in 1993. My career took me all over the world and introduced me to a lifestyle few will ever know. Shortly after going on active duty, I completed my master's degree, and several years later, I finished law school. I qualified to be a judge advocate general (JAG) lawyer but decided against a branch transfer from the military police corps. I had too much time in that branch and was having too much fun.

When I retired I decided to continue my law enforcement career as a civilian police chief. I completed the North Carolina Police Academy shortly after retiring and then moved to Georgia. I have been a police chief in Georgia almost continually since I retired. During that time, I attended and graduated from the FBI National Academy and the Georgia Israeli Law Enforcement Exchange. In 2009 I was appointed by Governor Sonny Perdue to serve on a major state board dealing with criminal justice. In July 2013, I was sworn in as president of the Georgia Association of Chiefs of Police. None of this success would have happened had I not taken that fork in the road so many years ago that led me to become an officer in the US Army. Perhaps my finest hour is yet to come. Who knows? But life until now has been pretty awesome, and just in case, the preparation continues every day. Thank you for reading my story.

CHAPTER 1

An Officer and a Gentleman

Chattanooga is a beautiful place even in December. It is an old city with a storied history and lots of charm. However, the city's location punctuates both its beauty and its drawbacks. The surrounding mountains trap the fumes from automobiles and industry that cause throat-burning smog and thick, gray clouds. But on this day, none of that matters. Even though it is raining, the air is clear, the sky is blue, and all is right with the world. And even if it's not, that's okay because today I am going to accomplish something that will change my life forever. I am on the way to my US Army commissioning ceremony, which is being held on the campus of the University of Tennessee at Chattanooga (UTC).

My wife, four-year-old son, and I are making the short trip down from Cleveland, Tennessee. My mother and uncle will drive from Alabama and meet us at the ceremony. I am wearing the same dress-green uniform I have worn every Wednesday for the last two years. But now there is a two-inch black piping down the leg of the pants. The patch indicating the rank of cadet first sergeant is gone from the jacket sleeve, and there is a circle of black piping at the bottom, indicating the uniform of a commissioned officer. Inside my front pants pocket is a shiny silver dollar at the ready for presentation to the first enlisted person from whom I receive a salute following my commissioning. This is an age-old tradition that goes back centuries, and one I certainly don't want to mess up. I can only imagine walking out from the ceremony as I meet one of the senior enlisted cadre who snaps me a smart military salute, offers his congratulations, and then holds out his hand, expecting the celebratory silver dollar. If I don't have one, there will be tremendous humiliation and embarrassment! So I check and recheck. It's still there, and I can relax.

There is a slight drizzle of rain coming down as we pull into the parking lot of the Guerry Student Center on UTC's campus. It is Saturday, so the lot is virtually empty, other than a couple of cars belonging to the ROTC cadre or fellow cadets also here for the ceremony. My wife and I rush to get our four-year-old out of the car and then run like mad for the door to keep from getting soaked. As a soon-to-be army officer, I am not allowed to carry an umbrella to keep the rain off. And since I have to be spit and polished for the event, we rush to our respective bathrooms to tidy up. As soon as we can collect ourselves and I am satisfied my uniform is perfect, it's time to find our way into the flag room of the Geurry Center.

UTC is a stately old school that was founded in 1886. Many of the buildings, both inside and out, are reflective of that era. The Guerry Center flag room is no exception. The walls are covered with thick oak paneling, and pictures of distinguished-looking school dignitaries and political figures line the walls. State flags stand along the walls, with the most important flag of all, the flag of the United States, taking center stage. In just a few minutes I will stand before that flag and swear an oath to protect it and the country it represents. There is seating for family members and loved ones set up on the open floor of the room. At the front of the room, chairs are lined up, facing the audience. These chairs are for the anxious, prospective second lieutenants of the University of Tennessee at Chattanooga Reserve Officers Training Corps.

There are six of us cadets who have bonded over the last two years, either by force or by choice. We are all from different backgrounds and social status, but we are all here for the same purpose: to serve our country and at the same time, to do our parts to make better lives for ourselves and families. Some, like me, have served before as enlisted soldiers, airmen, or sailors. We vary in age by several years, and I am the oldest cadet being commissioned. Some are barely in their twenties, have never held a job, and have no idea how the world really works. Hopefully, they will soon find out.

Also in attendance is Lieutenant Colonel Charles McGaw, the professor of military science for UTC. Colonel McGaw is an armor officer, better known as a "tanker" or "treadhead." He is a soft-spoken Texan, who is a true professional but doesn't take life too seriously. He and his cadre of officers and enlisted men have patiently taken a motley collection of male egos, testosterone, and braggadocio and turned them into a cohesive group of military men capable of becoming a true military asset.

Right on cue, I take my seat. After the usual introductory pleasantries and comments, the droning, meaningless babble of today's guest speaker begins. I have no idea what he said—or if he said anything, for that matter. I am too anxious and stoked to hear or care about anything except finally achieving the one thing I have been dreaming of for years. Reality has hit. In a few short minutes, if this guy will finish talking, I will stand, raise my right hand, swear the oath of a commissioned officer, and my wife and my mother will pin second lieutenant bars on my epaulettes. These special gold bars are the same ones used to commission my uncle Jack during the Korean War. It is an honor to follow in the footsteps of this fine soldier and war hero. As soon as the oath of office is complete, I will immediately transform from college student to "an officer and a gentleman."

As the guest speaker goes on and on about something I am sure would be important to our lives if we were listening, my mind begins to wander. I start to think about how I got here. Now being a commissioned officer in the military may not seem like a big deal to some. Each year the military commissions thousands of young men and women, usually without the least bit of fanfare. However, for me this is a validation. It is finally the recognition I have sought for so long and the satisfaction that something I have done in my life really matters. It is an achievement of immeasurable significance that will change my life forever and immediately propel me into not only another level of social recognition, but another level of acceptance as well. Basically, this ceremony will take a skinny, dirt poor, country bumpkin and give him a place in life that not everyone occupies. In my mind, at least, I will have arrived.

I will have spent twenty-seven years on this earth come January, and I have probably crammed more life into those years than most will in fifty. I begin to think about my life and all the adventures, narrow escapes, forks in the road, and interesting characters that have in one way or another contributed to my being here today.

CHAPTER 2

The Beginning

I was born in a tiny, ramshackle house in rural Alabama on January 22, 1947, to Ozia, a poor, unmarried, uneducated, country girl who already had one son to feed. The community was known as Whitehall. Back then in Alabama, communities usually got their names from either a church or cemetery, or both. Whitehall was no exception. It was so named because of Whitehall Methodist Church and Cemetery. The church was built in 1888 as a Presbyterian church, but it was purchased by the Methodists in 1920 and is still a functioning church. The cemetery was established in 1835 on land that was donated by John and Clara White. The cemetery and church became known as Whitehall.

Whitehall is an idyllic place. It is located in a beautiful valley between Lookout Mountain to the east and Sand Mountain to the west. US Highway 11 runs north and south through the community, and Will's Creek runs parallel to the highway. Numerous ridges run in every direction, and those ridges played a significant part in my childhood.

I lived with my grandfather, grandmother, mother, and older brother in this tiny shack of a house just off a dirt road, about a mile from the church. It was a sharecropper house, as that was what my grandfather did at the time. A sharecropper is someone who lives on a piece of land that belongs to someone else. He farms the land, buys seed, fertilizer, tools, mules, and the like, and when the crops come in, he gets half of the crop. The owner of the land and house gets the other half. Needless to say, there was not much crop to share, and times were hard.

I lived in the house I was born in until I was about nine months old. At that time, one of my uncles who was serving in the army bought a forty-acre piece of rock pasture with an old house on it. Incidentally, the little farm was located directly behind the Whitehall Cemetery. You had to walk through the cemetery to get to our house, and that walk could be really spooky at night. The story goes that two bachelor, bootlegging brothers built the house themselves and lived there for many years, making and selling moonshine liquor. There wasn't a straight or square board in that house.

When we first moved there, the floor consisted of boards laid across the dirt, and there were cracks in the walls big enough to put your hand through. Windows were large panes of glass held in with cement-like putty. One wood stove provided what little heat we had, and another stove in the kitchen was used to cook our meals. Of course, there were no bathrooms or running water.

Our "bathroom" was a privy, or outhouse, way out in the backyard. An outhouse is called an outhouse for a reason, and it is located out there for a reason too; it stinks to high heaven. And since the outhouse is a long way off, most folks don't like to get up in the middle of the night and walk that far in the cold. Most people kept a "slop jar" (also called a "thunder pot" by some) under the bed. Now for city folk or the otherwise uninformed, a slop jar is basically a bucket you use for a toilet. Some slop jars were just plain buckets, while some were more elaborate and made out of enameled steel. It is kept under the bed until the morning when, hopefully, it is emptied.

There was no electricity. This was uncommon even for this period, as most folks around had it. But it certainly wasn't uncommon for my family, since they didn't believe in anything modern. Light for the house came from two kerosene lamps, which gave off about as much light as a match. Imagine trying to read or do homework by such a tiny light source. It is small wonder I am not totally blind. Years later, my uncle had the house wired for electricity. My grandfather had no concept of electricity and went around the house, putting tape over the outlets to keep the electricity from getting out.

A few years later, someone jacked up the house and put in a real floor. It didn't help all that much, just made it a little easier to clean. There were four rooms in the house. There was a living room and dining room combination, a kitchen, and two small bedrooms. For years my mother and I shared a bed, while my brother slept in another bed in the same room. Dad (my grandfather) and Nanny had the other bedroom. There were no closets in any of these rooms. Dad and Nanny both had big old trunks where they kept most of their clothes. Nanny had a "shifrobe," where she hung her hang-up clothes. A shifrobe is another Alabama mispronunciation and is actually a "chiffarobe," but what you grow up with tends to be the way it stays.

There were wide cracks in the walls and around the window frames. Newspapers were used as sort of a wallpaper to cover them. Nanny would make glue out of flour and water and stick the paper to the walls.

Our water came from a deep well that was drilled on the property. The one good thing about the well was that it had some of the best water I have ever tasted. It came out of the well ice cold and pure as mountain snow. The only problem was getting it out of the well, which was usually my job. The well was 150 feet deep. The mechanism for extracting the water was a homemade windlass, made from a smoothed-out round log, with an iron handle through it and a long rope with a special bucket on the end. This was somehow attached to an old, falling-in well house. When the bucket was lowered and hit the water, a valve opened on one end of the bucket, allowing it to fill with water. When the bucket was full and you started cranking the windless, the valve closed and kept the water in. One hundred and fifty feet later, you had a bucket of fresh water. The water was then transferred from the well bucket into one used for the house. Water was dispensed from the bucket with a dipper, and since we were a family of five with only one dipper, you had to get used to drinking after each other. This wasn't a problem as long as it was just us. The problem was when strangers or outside family came to visit. No one in my family had sense enough to simply dip the water into a glass and drink from that. That was an extra step and a waste of time.

We lived six miles from the nearest town of any size and eight miles from one that carried the supplies we needed to survive. Because of this, and the fact my mother and grandparents had lived through the Depression and other tough times, nothing was ever wasted. Nails were bent straight and recycled. Thread taken from the tops of flour and feed sacks was rolled into balls, and every scrap of cloth was saved for use as something. Flour and feed sacks were used to make shirts and dresses. Smart milling companies even started selling their flour in sacks with prints on them, so a pretty dress or shirt could be sewn from them. My grandmother went to the extreme of even saving foil chewing gum wrappers. I never figured out what she thought she might do with them. She just couldn't throw anything away.

CHAPTER 3

Ozia

I wrote earlier that my mother was unmarried when I was born. Keep in mind this was in 1947, and at that time, unwed pregnancy was taboo, and girls did whatever they could to avoid it. My mother never married, and I never knew who my father was. This was especially traumatic for a child unfortunate enough to be born into such circumstances. I guess in a way I became a poster child for prolife, since the easy thing to do would have been to abort me or give me up for adoption. Fortunately, my mother was having none of that and stuck it out.

Not having a father really didn't bother me until I started to school. Until that point, it had not really hit home that I was all that different from everyone else. School changed all that. There were times when I was teased unmercifully by older kids and even kids in my own class. One boy, who was a couple years older than I, asked me one day who my daddy was. When I told him I didn't have a daddy, he remarked, "Everybody's got a daddy. Where did you come from, under a rock?" I could only stand there and fight back tears as he said it. His comments really stung and hurt my feelings terribly. However, I learned years later, while I was on active duty, he had enlisted in the army and was stationed where I happened to be at the time. I looked him up and paid a visit. The look on his face when he saw I was a commissioned officer was priceless. Plus, he had to salute me. There is justice after all.

The most traumatic thing of all for me was when the teachers had the class stand one at a time at the beginning of the year and tell all sorts of personal things about ourselves. They always wanted you to say who your mother and father were and what they did. I never figured out what that had to do with anything, and I hated it. Every year I dreaded that worse than any other aspect of going to school, and I thought of all sorts of ways to answer the question about my father. Of course, none were very good, and I even had at least one teacher question me further when I said I didn't have a daddy. She wanted to know if my mother was divorced or if my daddy was dead. It's not that they were being mean; it was just the attitude people had about the subject at the time. Today, who cares?

One of very few regrets I have is that I didn't sit down with my mother in later years and press her to tell me. Maybe it is for the best. Maybe I wasn't supposed to know. Now it really doesn't matter as much as it once did, but I still regret not finding out. Several years ago, I went on a quest to find out about my father and pestered several people I thought might know. But nothing turned up. My mother was a strange person and kept things close to her vest. She may very well have gone all through life and never told anyone, no matter how close they were.

My mother was also not married when my brother, Dale, was born eight years earlier. One thing is for sure. We are from two different daddies, and we are as different as night is from day. Looks, mannerisms, drive, the whole bit; we are totally different. The one big difference, besides our looks, was that he had a name on his birth certificate indicating who his father was. I am not sure who this person was, nor do I know anything about him. But the name she listed as the father was M. B. Ott. I remember seeing some old letters she kept in a trunk that were from someone by that name, but I don't remember where they were from or any other information. My mother never mentioned his name, nor did anyone else in the family. It was like he was a phantom or ghost.

I do know this about my own birth. Many years ago, I found a letter in that same trunk written to my mother by one of my uncles. He was serving in the air force and was stationed at Sheppard Air Force Base, Texas. The letter was of no special significance, and its contents were simply a brother writing his sister. However, the letter was postmarked sometime in December 1946 and was sent to an address in Indianapolis, Indiana. Since I was born in January of 1947, there is a good chance I was actually born in Indiana. Who knows? My birth certificate was not filed until several months after I was born, and it simply says I was born at home, which was common during that time. I know my mother spent some time in Indianapolis because a distant cousin lived there. I remember hearing about her working at a Woolworth's store there, so she may have gone up to have me and then returned home sometime later. This certainly would have explained her trip there. As I have already said, she did not like to venture off, and a trip such as this would have been highly unusual. Unfortunately, I lost the envelope from the letter over the years and have no address to check. So another dead end, I suppose.

My mother was a unique individual, and to say she was strange would be putting it mildly. She was born in 1918 and was the only girl among four boys. She was born to Nancy Jane and Douglas Doddwick, my maternal grandparents. Mother's name is very unusual, and I have never heard of anyone else with a similar name. The story I heard was that a school chum of my grandmother's was named Ozia, and my mother was named after her. I guess that since she was a girl, they didn't waste time finding a middle name. She was called Ode her entire life by everyone who knew her.

Mother was a beautiful woman, with jet-black hair that had a natural wave. She had piercing green eyes and was, in short, a head turner. She may have had a sixth-grade education if that. I never heard her speak of going to school, and any school pictures of her that I ever saw went no further than the sixth grade. She was, however, an avid reader and read everything she could find. Out in the country, reading is about the only form of entertainment available, so she made good use of it. Besides loving me, the one good thing my mother did for me was to read to me. I spent hours lying in bed, listening to her read the same stories to me over and over. Books in those days were hard to come by and were usually hand-me-downs from someone else.

Our most read book was really a series of small booklets sewn together. The series was the *Uncle Wiggly* adventures by Howard R. Garis. They were about an elderly gentleman rabbit that traveled around the country, getting into all sorts of trouble. After a year or so of listening to mother read these stories, I started reading along with her, and on occasion, I would be reading ahead of her. I never remember learning to read. I just always knew how, and when I started first grade, I could read at the third-grade level or higher. I was so far ahead of my first-grade classmates that I skipped the second grade and went directly to the third grade. I could count to one hundred, tell time, and do simple math, including the "times tables." I learned to tell time and count by reading Sears and Roebuck catalogs, which were a household staple at the time. Even my family had one. Mother pointed to the clocks and watches for sale and explained what time the watch or clock showed. Somehow her crude methods taught me how to tell time. I learned simple math by looking at the various things for sale and counting them. Subtraction was simply taking something away. Amazingly, when I started first grade, the teacher used basically the same methods.

Several years later, my mother bought me a full set of *Funk and Wagnalls* encyclopedias. I have no idea of what possessed her to get them, but I am sure glad she did. She bought them from the local A&P grocery store that ran a promotion allowing a customer to buy one volume for each $10 worth of groceries purchased. I think the volumes were about $1 each, and it took her a long time to get the set. These books opened up the world to me, and I cannot count the things I learned to do from these books. I learned to drive a car, for example. I learned Morse code, and I learned about electricity long before we had it. All from a set of books. After I left home to go into the navy, my mother gave the books to a coworker for her daughter to use. I really didn't pay much attention to the fact they were gone until many years later, after I had become an army officer and mother had passed away. I decided to try to find them, so I called a couple of people she worked with at the laundry. Lo and behold, someone knew who had them. A quick phone call to the daughter of the coworker turned up the books, and she was gracious enough to return them to me. I was as excited as a child on Christmas Day when the box arrived. Today these treasured books occupy a select spot in my study. It is easy to tell what subjects held my attention the most from the discoloration of the page fronts in the area of the subject matter. For example, you can look at the M volume and see a dark line down the middle of the book. If you open the volume at that mark you will be at "Morse code." If you wanted that information today, you would simply google it on a computer. But back then, this was high-speed stuff, and I felt the whole world was mine for the looking.

My mother was not worldly at all, and for whatever reason, was afraid to try new things or venture very far from what she knew or what she was familiar with. For the first few years of my life, she basically worked as farm labor either at our little farm or for a larger operation that needed hands to pick cotton. One of my earliest memories is of getting dressed early in the morning and waiting in the cold for a big ole truck to pull up in front of the house. We would clamber up into the bed, along with several others who had been picked up elsewhere, and bounce along miles of dirt roads until we got to the cotton fields. There everyone would get out, drag their pick sacks across the field, and start the arduous task of picking the thousands of cotton bolls needed to fill the sack. My task was to stay out of her way and not get into anything while she worked. I was too young to pick, so I usually sat under a tree somewhere or slept until lunch or when it was time to get back on the truck to head home.

At the time, cotton-picking paid about one dollar per hundred pounds, and a good picker could pick two to three hundred pounds a day. Picking cotton is without a doubt the hardest work I have ever done. It is backbreaking and very hard on one's fingers. But when there is no other way to get a little money, it is better than nothing. During this time, there was no welfare, public housing, or food stamps. If you ate, you worked for it.

Several years later, when I was about seven or eight, Mother went to work at a laundry in Fort Payne, about eight miles from Whitehall. This was a major move for her, as she didn't like being around people very much and was reluctant to try anything outside her comfort zone. She worked at the laundry for twenty-seven years, pressing clothes and sheets in terrible heat and under substandard working conditions. She never complained one time about how hard she worked. She just did it. She had an opportunity once to change jobs when a well-known shirt manufacturer located a plant close to Fort Payne. The plant paid considerably more than she would ever make at the laundry with much better benefits. Lots of people, including me, tried to encourage her to take the job, but she was afraid to leave what she had and stayed put.

My mother had so many quirks and personality issues it is hard to begin to describe her. She loved me dearly but was overly protective and possessive. I missed many opportunities in my earlier years because of this. I never figured out if she was simply afraid I would get hurt doing something or if she was jealous of my time away from her. When I was ten or so, I wanted terribly to join the Boy Scouts. There was a troop forming at Valley Head, and most of my classmates were in it. They came to school after a weekend with all sorts of stories about their adventures and scouting activities. But no matter how many times I asked her, she would not let me join. Looking back, the only thing I can figure is that she was jealous because by this time, I was roaming the ridges alone, miles from our house. I just think she was possessive of my time and wanted it all to herself. Maybe she was afraid I would become aware of the world and leave her. Who knows?

To say she was stubborn would be an understatement. If she didn't like something or was reluctant to try something, that was it. You couldn't budge her with dynamite. Once she made up her mind, there was no changing it, period. The most troublesome thing about her was that she could hate someone immediately for no reason. She would just look at someone and say, "I don't like that person." You could ask her why, and she could not tell you. She would only say, "I just don't like them." No reason was needed, and she would not change her mind. Of course she came by this honestly, as both my grandparents were the same way.

When I began dating, if I started to act serious about a girl, that would be it. Mother had no more use for her. As long as it was a date or two, things were fine. But after three or so, she started to find all sorts of things wrong with the girl. If I got really serious, she would start doing things to try to break us up. She had the same attitude toward my older brother, Dale, when it came to women. When we first moved to Fort Payne, we lived in a rundown little shack of a duplex. We lived in one side, and another family lived in the other. While we were there, a lady named Evelyn and her two daughters moved in on the other side. Things were great. She and my mother became very close and even went out together a time or two. They had a lot in common and had similar interests, but that all changed when my brother came back to Alabama and moved in with us.

Dale started hanging out at her place, and he and Evelyn eventually started dating. At that point, Mother had no more use for Evelyn, and just like that, she hated everything about her. There were no more conversations or anything. It was over. Dale eventually married her, and they moved away. I liked Evelyn a lot and spent many nights at their house. I got along with her two daughters, as well. The oldest was only a year or two younger than I was, and we were more like brother and sister than uncle and niece. We even double-dated a few times later on.

There was no reason for Mother to treat Evelyn like she did other than jealousy. They had never had a cross word before Evelyn and Dale got married, but Mother hated her anyway. Dale tried a time or two to talk to her, but she was having none of it. She made it very clear Evelyn was not welcome in her house. Dale told her if his wife was not welcome, he wasn't either. He turned and left and never spoke to her again. Mother and Dale did not speak one word to each other for over twenty years, and they avoided each other at all cost. When I came around, Mother tried to use me and to come between Dale and me. We had some pretty strong words about it, but that didn't change anything. These were two of the most stubborn people who ever drew a breath, and neither was going to give an inch. I had to side with Dale somewhat because what she was doing was totally wrong and undeserved.

I had a friend while I was on the *Saratoga* who was also from

Alabama, and he and I became quite close. He came home with me a couple of times, and I visited his house once or twice. He was a very nice guy, and we had a lot in common, so I introduced him to my niece. They hit it off right away and dated for a while when he could come home with me. Mother liked him fine until she found out that he was dating Sherry, and then that was it. She ordered him out of our house and told him to never come back. This all came out of the blue, and I was terribly embarrassed. I didn't come home for a long time after that and didn't speak to her for over a year.

When I first started dating the girl I eventually married, my mother could not have cared less. It was only when she found out we were going to get married that she went ballistic. She said all sorts of mean things about Bernice and even said if we married, we would have "retarded children." We had planned to marry on Christmas Eve and had the wedding arranged at a local church. I did not tell Mother anything about the wedding because I knew she would never agree to it. In Alabama at the time, there was a law that required the male to be twenty-one years of age in order to marry. The female only had to be eighteen, and since I was only eighteen at the time, this was a problem. For me to marry required a parent to sign papers allowing the marriage. And since I knew my mother would never sign them, my brother and I concocted a plan whereby he would sign as my guardian. We went down to the courthouse to get the license and told the lady at the window our mother had abandoned us at a railroad depot when we were small. We went on and on about living on the streets, begging for food and how my brother had to raise me. My fiancé and sister-in-law were around the corner within earshot of our story. They were laughing so hard I was sure they were going to give us away. By the time we got the license, the women working there were all crying their eyes out at our sad story.

On the twenty-first of December, my brother came rushing in and told me our mother had found out about our plans and was threatening to have the marriage annulled. She was also threatening to show up at the church and cause a big scene. There was nothing for us to do except move the wedding up a few days. We called the preacher and told him we needed to get married that night. He cautiously agreed and said to come over now. We got married at his house at ten o'clock at night, with only the preacher, his wife, and my brother and his wife in attendance. There was no music, no bouquet, and no wedding dress. Her dress was being fitted at the seamstress shop, so we got married without it. My mother did not speak to us for almost a year and hated my wife for years after that. Her attitude toward all of us changed when my son was born five years after we got married. From that moment on, all was good. She wound up worshipping the grandson she had said earlier would be "retarded."

CHAPTER 4

Uncle Doug and Aunt Nancy

My grandparents were affectionately known to all as Uncle Doug and Aunt Nancy. I called my grandmother "Nanny" and my grandfather "Dad." I guess in a way, he was the closest thing to a dad I ever knew, even though he didn't feel that way about me. My grandmother was a tiny woman, maybe five feet tall, if that, and probably didn't weigh eighty pounds soaking wet. She always wore an old, homemade apron and a bonnet every day. She had long hair that she wore up in what she called a "doo knob." To look at her, one would never imagine there was that much hair on her head, but when she took it down, it reached all the way to the floor. She was probably the meanest woman I ever knew. I'm not talking about just being mean to me; she was evil. She hated anything and everything, usually for no reason. She hated people she didn't even know and things she didn't know anything about.

I used to think she could put a spell on someone, and I am not too sure that she couldn't. She was sort of a medicine woman and could cure almost anything. None of us ever went to a doctor because she knew all sorts of potions, poultices, and homemade remedies to cure or fix every sort of ailment. She could knock a cold out in two days or less with her homemade cough remedy. Of course her "cough medicine" was peppermint stick candy and corn whiskey, but it worked.

One time my brother was riding our old workhorse, Charley, when Charley decided it was time to go back to the barn. Dale was riding bareback, since we didn't own a saddle, and was just barely hanging on when Charley ran him at a full gallop under my grandmother's clothesline. Needless to say, Dale took a couple turns around the line and smacked into the ground pretty hard, breaking his right arm. He came into the house whining and crying, holding his arm. My grandmother sat him down and stretched his arm out until the bone was reset. She then took some brown paper from a grocery bag, soaked it in homemade vinegar, and wrapped it around his arm, making sort of a cast. She took an old dish towel and fashioned it into a sling. He wore that around a couple of days, until she took off the paper and vinegar. His arm was as good as new, and he never went to the doctor.

Another time I jumped off a foot log into a creek and landed on a piece of wood with a nail sticking up. The nail went completely through my foot, and I had to hold the board down with one foot and pull up until the nail came out. I hobbled off home with a big hole in my foot. As soon as I got home, my grandmother got one of the kerosene lamps down and emptied the kerosene into a pan. She took my foot and plopped it right into the kerosene and made me soak it for several minutes. She then took my foot out, dried it off, wrapped a cloth around it, and sent me on my way. After that, she poured the kerosene back into the lamp. My grandmother didn't waste anything ever, especially not kerosene.

When I was real young, perhaps two or three years old, I fell off a stool onto our red-hot heater. As I have mentioned earlier, we heated the house with either a wood- or coal-burning stove. When the fire really got going, the heater would turn red-hot. How we kept from burning down that old house is a miracle. We had an old three-legged stool that Dad probably handmade. The stool really didn't have a purpose, but no one would throw it out. I would sit on it by the fire to get warm. One day it was particularly cold, and the stove was red-hot. I was sitting on that wobbly stool when it toppled over, dumping me right onto the stove. I landed on my cheek, leaving half my face on the side of the heater. The first thing my mother and Nanny did was to soak my face in butter and give me a tablespoon of paregoric, which is an opium-based pain medicine. They repeated this treatment over the next several days, and, of course, I never went to see a doctor. For years afterward, I had a terrible scar on the left side of my face. Fortunately, as years went by, the scar became smaller and smaller. Now, unless you know it is there, you can't see it.

If you had a boil or other ailment somewhere on your body, Nanny would take a potato and make a poultice out of it. She would split the potato and then take a spoon and scrape the white "meat" of the potato onto a piece of cloth. The cloth was placed over the affected area, and within a day, the affliction would be cured. This was true for sties, splinters, sprains, and most other physical ailments. A good potato poultice would fix it right up. Another useful remedy was to mix a small amount of kerosene with powdered sulfur. This was given for extreme coughs, such as whooping cough. The taste alone would cure you. Vinegar was mixed with baking soda for relief of upset stomach or indigestion. One of very few store-bought medicines she used was Syrup of Black Draught, which was a laxative.

Nanny was equally adept at treating our animals for whatever ailments they might have. Now when I say our animals, I mean our one milk cow or our workhorse. On rare occasions, we might have a hog being fattened up for slaughter, but that was it. She went into the woods and found all sorts of plants and vegetation that could be used for medicine. I would give anything if video cameras had been around during her lifetime so that some of her mountain knowledge could have been captured. None of what she knew was ever written down. It was all in her head. If a cow went into "season," meaning she was ready to breed, there were plants that she would gather for the cow. If a cow went "dry," meaning she quit giving milk, my grandmother had a remedy for that, too.

Nanny, on the surface and to the unknowing, was this kind, gentle, little, old lady who everybody loved. Remember, she was "Aunt Nancy" to everyone. What they didn't see was the real Nanny. This Nanny would hide candy from me. This Nanny would treat me like a stranger, but when any of my cousins came, she would lay on the charm and be the perfect grandmother. She would sit and talk to them for hours about what they had been doing. How is school? What do you want Santa to bring you? And on and on and on. And that candy she hid from me was handed out like that was what she did all the time. Of course I didn't understand and wondered, *What have they got that I don't have? How do I get attention like they do?* It never came. I always felt like I was a burden and an extra mouth to feed. No matter how hard I tried, I couldn't get that attention. It may sound like I was just jealous or being childish, but when you are three, four, or five years old, you don't understand why you are not loved or wanted.

One time I remember a guy coming to the house to see my mother. He made the mistake of driving his car up to the house and taking her for a walk somewhere. Both Nanny and Dad hated anyone who dared "come calling" on Mother. I never knew the reason. I don't know if it was jealousy, control, or what, but men were not welcome at our house when it came to Mother. So on this particular day, some unsuspecting fool dared enter the sacred yard and took my mother away for a few minutes. While they were gone, Nanny dragged me into her little scheme of teaching this poor guy a lesson. She had me find a board and some nails and then place the board with the nails under the tires of his car. When they returned a short time later and he drove off—bang! Flat tire! I was maybe six or so but old enough to know this wasn't right. But I had no choice at the time.

One interesting thing about Nanny was that although she only had a fourth-grade education, she could work the most complex crossword puzzles she could find. She had really poor eyesight and besides wearing really thick glasses, used a magnifying glass to read. She would sit in her rocking chair, rocking back and forth, hold the magnifying glass up to read the clue, and then put the magnifying glass down and write in the answer. I think the only good thing I got from her was my love for crossword puzzles.

Like my grandfather, Nanny was hardworking. Both got up early every morning, and their day began right away. She would start the day by building a fire in the wood cookstove before going out to the barn to milk the cow. All this happened way before daylight, and there were no lights in the barn or on the path to the barn. It seemed like she and the old cow just had a relationship, and she was able to get the job done by feel. She milked the cow, left some feed for her, and brought the pail of milk to the house for processing. After the milk sat for a few minutes, she separated the cream from the top of the milk. The cream was stored in another jug and allowed to clabber. Clabber is another way of saying "spoiled." The milk literally separates into curds and whey, and when it completely clabbers, it is ready to churn into butter. The milk was poured into glass jugs to be stored in our milk cellar. We didn't have electricity or any other way to keep things cool, so big holes were dug fairly deep into the ground and filled with cold water from the well. The jugs of milk were lowered into the holes and kept there until needed. This primitive cooling method was better than nothing, as milk sours fairly quickly. I have a significant scar across the bridge of my nose from walking up behind my brother one day as he was digging a milk cellar. I was maybe two years old, and he didn't see me come up behind him. He swung the shovel back with a load of dirt and almost cut off my nose. No doctor, of course. Nanny to the rescue!

When the milk processing was complete and Nanny was waiting for the cream to finish clabbering, it was time to start breakfast, as Dad would be ready to eat shortly. Breakfast was always the same: eggs, biscuits, and white gravy. White gravy is made from lard or bacon grease mixed with flour in a skillet. When the mixture starts to cook, milk is poured into the skillet and stirred until it thickens into gravy. On occasion, there might be sausage or bacon, and there was always plenty of homemade jelly or jam to go along with the biscuits. Most of the time, we had a can of sorghum syrup on hand. Every now and then, particularly in the winter, Nanny made oatmeal. This was usually served when eggs or other staples were scarce. Oats were particularly suited to our needs because they lasted forever and needed no refrigeration. Since there was no electricity, and certainly no microwave, leftover oatmeal was eaten cold. Hey, if you are hungry, it ain't bad.

Dad always sat down first. He didn't care who was visiting; he sat down at the table first and immediately started eating. Dad always referred to biscuits as "catheads." I have no idea where this came from other than the possibility they might resemble a cat's head in appearance. Nevertheless, catheads they were. Nanny also had a big pot of coffee percolating on the stove. Dad drank lots of coffee and wanted it a certain way. He poured the coffee into his cup and then filled it half full with cane sugar. He never figured out that he could use lots less sugar if he stirred it. When he finished eating, there would be two inches of sugar left in the cup. After eating his fill of eggs and gravy, he often took a biscuit and broke it apart into a saucer. He then poured coffee over the biscuit and ate it like a pudding. He usually drank his coffee from the saucer as well, adding more sugar each time he filled the cup.

One interesting aspect of my childhood and upbringing was that even though we were poor "white trash," so to speak, I was taught manners from an early age. You would never sit at Nanny's table with a hat on, no matter who you were. Even Dad removed his old, tattered fedora before he sat down. "Please" and "thank you" were the norm when eating, and when you were finished, you asked to be excused. Dad usually ignored this particular rule because he got up whenever he got ready. But it certainly applied to everyone else. Dad's favorite line when company sat at the table was, "If you don't like what's here, don't mess over it, 'cause we got to eat it."

When breakfast was done and dishes washed, it was time to start cooking the evening meal or canning. Wood stoves take a long time to get hot, and there is no such thing as a little hot. They are either ready or they are not. And they use a lot of wood, so you don't want to waste a good fire. The fire that cooked breakfast had to be used for other chores as well. So Nanny might put on a big pot of stew or soup, based on what was available, and would probably put on a couple of pones of cornbread. Sometimes she baked a cake or a pie, and depending on what time of the year it was, she might start the process for canning vegetables or fruit. Nanny did not waste anything, so everything was used for something sooner or later.

Canning involved getting the fruit or vegetables ready, which meant peeling, coring, washing, and so on. While she was preparing these, water was heating in her pressure cooker on the stove. When all the prep was complete and the water hot enough, she put the food that was to be canned into mason jars and placed rubber rings and lids on the jars. If the canning involved fruit, she sealed the jar with a layer of paraffin. This supposedly prevented mold from getting onto the mixture. She then put the lid on the cooker and watched the gauge on top to make sure it didn't get too high and explode. The stove was now full. All stove eyes had something cooking on them, and the oven was full. Many times she would make a cornbread mixture and cook hoecakes on the stovetop, between the eyes. She just poured it right onto the stove. By now, the cream was sufficiently clabbered and it was time to churn butter.

A churn is a big earthen crock with a wood or ceramic top that has a hole in the middle. A dasher goes into the churn, with the handle going through the hole. A dasher is a round piece of wood that is longer than the depth of the churn, with two pieces of wood attached to the end in a cross-wise manner. The clabber is poured into the churn, and the person doing the churning pushes the dasher down into the mix. Up and down goes the dasher as fast as the person can make it go. The dasher action separates the cream from the curds and whey, and it becomes butter. This process takes from several minutes to an hour. Once the butter separates, it comes to the top of the mixture. It is then scraped into a bowl and kneaded to remove any liquid trapped inside the butter. The remaining liquid becomes one of my favorite foods, buttermilk. I can eat my weight in buttermilk and cornbread, which is strange because buttermilk is basically spoiled milk that is beaten back into a liquid.

At least one day a week was washday, which was an adventure in itself. Outside the house was a fire pit with a big, cast iron wash pot over it. Nanny filled the pot with water I had drawn from the well and lit a fire under it. When the water started boiling, she put all our clothes into the pot, along with some homemade soap. When the clothes had boiled for several minutes, she would use a long hickory pole to take them out of the pot and put them into the rinse water. When the clothes had rinsed, we wrung them out as best we could and hung them on the clothesline to dry in the sun. Later in the day, when they were sufficiently dry, she took them down and started ironing, using the flat irons that had been heating on the top of the same cookstove.

Many times when the canning or other cooking was done, Nanny got out her quilting frame and worked on a quilt. She didn't waste anything, so many quilts were made from scraps and rags pieced together. I guess if it's cold enough, you don't care what the quilt is made of as long as it's warm. She did on occasion make quilts from piecework patterns. For these quilts she carefully cut pieces of cloth using a pattern. These pattern pieces were sewn together and then quilted with batting cloth in the middle. Many of her quilts were very decorative and attractive. This effort also provided a very warm cover for winter nights.

One good thing I can say about growing up at Whitehall was that I never went hungry. Nanny always grew a large garden that produced plenty of vegetables, which were either eaten fresh or canned for later use. She planted rows and rows of cabbage, which she chopped up finely for sauerkraut or used in homemade soup. Tomatoes were used to make soup, canned whole, or used to make homemade catsup. Homemade pickles, chow chow, and hot peppers made any meal tastier, regardless of what it was. A fairly large fruit orchard supplied apples, pears, plums, and peaches. I spent many an afternoon high up in an apple tree with a good book, munching away on the greenest apples that I could find. Nanny found this extremely upsetting because I ate so many of them. She fussed that I wouldn't wait for them to ripen before I ate them. I just loved green apples, I guess. We also kept a strawberry patch and grape arbor.

There was always a chicken coop, and laying hens roamed everywhere around the house. Every now and then, especially if company were coming, she would go out in the yard and catch a rooster. Once she had him in her grasp, she spun him around and around, until she wrung his neck off. The old rooster flopped around the yard, spraying blood everywhere. She cleaned it, cut it up, and presto, fried chicken was on the table that night. Nanny cooked everything from scratch and always the same way. She never experimented or tried to learn to cook anything she wasn't used to or with which she was unfamiliar.

We had our own corn ground at a grist mill, and the meal was stored in the meal bin. Flour was store bought and kept in the flour bin. You had to sift both before using because the cornmeal had corn husks in it, and the flour had tiny little weevils, neither of which was very appetizing.

Cornbread was an everyday staple and, of course, made from scratch. Today, making cornbread is simple. You just buy some self-rising cornmeal mix, add buttermilk, and bake. Back then it was not so simple. You had to sift the meal and add sifted flour. Then add a pinch of salt, a pinch of baking soda, a teaspoon of Clabber Girl baking powder, one egg, and buttermilk. If any of the ingredients were off, the bread didn't taste right, and Dad would be mad. Too much baking soda left the bread sour, with yellow specks in it. Too much salt brought obvious results. Too little, and the bread tasted flat. Too little baking powder, and the bread wouldn't rise properly. Too much, and it became a cornmeal pound cake. Add to this the uncertainty of the woodstove heat, and you can see what an ordeal cooking was back then. Imagine trying to bake a cake!

Store-bought goods were always things we didn't grow ourselves or would keep for a long time without refrigeration. Dad loved Vienna sausages and usually kept some hidden away. Of course, the Alabama pronunciation is "vy-eener," and I didn't know the difference until I was grown. These little jewels lasted forever, and a can could make a meal for one person. Canned salmon was another staple for the same reason. You could keep it forever and make several tasty dishes out of it.

We always grew a crop of corn when I was a kid. Corn was mainly used as feed for the livestock, but some of it was used to feed us, as well. When the corn first came in, we gathered the young ears for cooking. These were called "roas'nears" by country people. The correct pronunciation was "roasting ears," but we, of course, shortened it up a bit. We threw the ears right into the oven, husk and all, and let them cook for several minutes. When they were done, we ate the corn right off the cob.

Nanny made homemade hominy when the rest of the corn crop came in. Hominy is puffed corn that has the hull removed. You remove it by soaking the corn in lye. Most of the time she mixed a small amount of Red Devil lye, which was one of the few things that were store bought, with water. If she didn't have lye from the store, she would make her own by pouring water over cold ashes from the wash pit. The runoff water contained enough lye to get the job done. The corn was allowed to marinate for several minutes, until the hulls came off. Then the remaining corn was boiled. Once the hominy was done, she either served it boiled with butter or fried it in a skillet. Either way it is good. Sometimes she would can the hominy for later.

Grits have always been a Southern staple and are made from ground hominy. For some unknown reason, we never ate grits. I didn't know what they were until I joined the military.

Another Nanny staple was poke salad. Poke salad is a wild vegetable that grows all over the South. It grows as a stalk and can get seven or eight feet tall if left alone. It produces bright red berries that are poisonous. The only edible parts of poke salad are the very young and tender shoots that are close to the ground. These shoots are cleaned and cooked just like turnip greens or collards. Throw in a slice of fatback or bacon, and you have a real treat. Poke salad has kept many country kids from going hungry, including me.

About every other year or so, we killed and butchered a hog. This was an adventure in itself that involved several people and usually a distant neighbor, who came by to help in exchange for some of the meat. Dad or my brother went out with the little twenty-two that I had fixed and shot the old hog behind the ear. It was then hoisted by the hind feet, gutted, and drained. Then it was butchered, with some of the meat being saved for homemade sausage and the rest cut for smoking or curing.

Nanny didn't waste anything, remember? The same was true for hog meat. She used every possible part of the hog for something. We even ate scrambled hog brains with eggs for breakfast. Various organs and lesser cuts of meat were used to make souse meat or, what some people call hog-head cheese. The meat is finely ground and mixed with hot peppers and vinegar. It is actually not that bad, especially if you are hungry enough. The only thing Nanny would not use from the hog was the intestines. She was not into chitterlings. She did cook pig's ears, pig's feet, and pig's tail.

Most of the meat was smoked and sugar-cured in order to keep it without refrigeration. Certain cuts of the pork were set aside for sausage. The sausage was ground up with an old, hand-cranked sausage grinder. The meat had to be cut small enough to fit down into the mouth of the grinder. The crank worked a cutting device that forced the meat out through openings in the front. This was tiresome work, and sausage making usually took all of one day or more to get done. Once the meat was ground to her liking, Nanny added her recipe of spices, making the sausage just the right hotness for Dad. Sage, cayenne pepper, and salt were the usual additions. The mix was kneaded over and over, until she was satisfied the spices were thoroughly blended in.

The problem with any of the cuts of meat that weren't cured or smoked was that they didn't keep very well without being refrigerated. So we had to eat them fast before they spoiled. I can remember eating raw bacon or fatback when I was really small. Nanny probably gave it to me to keep me quiet while she cooked, but for whatever reason, it was good to me. If you ate raw pork today, you might be sick as a dog, but back then, it was a normal thing, I suppose.

When all of the hog had been cut up, some of the lard (hog fat) was set aside to make lye soap. For many years, Nanny made the only soap that we used, whether to bathe with or to wash clothes. She boiled the hog fat down and then added lye to the mixture and poured it into a shallow pan. Once it cooled, she cut the soap into square bars. Some of the bars were shaved into fine powder to be used for washing clothes.

The skin of the hog was often deep-fried in lard and made into cracklings. Sometimes she mixed the cracklings with her cornbread for crackling bread.

Like I said, Nanny didn't waste anything, especially when it could be eaten. One of the better treats she cooked up was sassafras tea. Sassafras is a small tree that grows wild out in the country, and the roots can be used for tea. She would go out into the woods, identify a tree, and dig up the roots. Sassafras roots are bright red and have a sweet, pungent smell to them. She brought the roots home, cleaned off the dirt, and boiled them. As the roots boil, they *really* turned red. When the roots had boiled enough, she added a small amount of sugar. The result was sweet, tasty sassafras tea. The original root beer was simply sassafras tea with carbonated water.

Nanny and Dad together were a sight to see. Neither talked very much, especially not to each other. I can never remember having a conversation with either of them in the fifteen or so years I lived with them. And I can never remember a conversation between the two of them. They just didn't communicate, and there were no outward signs of affection. I never saw them kiss, hold hands, cuddle, or anything else that indicated they cared for each other. Every once in a while, she would get mad at him over some trivial thing and pout for days. If she got really mad, she would put on her one good dress and hat, put some spare clothes in a paper sack, and head down to the highway to catch the Greyhound bus. Nanny was on her way to Arkansas.

Nanny was born and raised in Guy, Arkansas. The story I always heard was that my grandfather went to Arkansas in a wagon and brought her back to Alabama. Nanny had been married before and was divorced. My grandfather supposedly was in Arkansas for some unknown reason, and the story went that he was walking down the street in Guy and saw her. I suppose a short romance ensued, and he came back for her a short time later in the wagon.

Anytime Nanny got mad, she ran off back home. She stayed just long enough for him to start missing her cooking and then she would come straggling back in. When Nanny came back, there was never any kissing or making up and certainly no, "I am sorry." They would just start right back as if nothing had ever happened.

Nanny had a close sister named Anna back in Guy. Her last name was Mode, and the Alabama pronunciation of her name was "Anner" Mode. Anner was a big, fat, boisterous lady, totally different from Nanny. On occasion, she would come to Alabama for a visit, and when she did, I hated it. She was bossy and obnoxious. She treated me like a second-class child because I am sure that Nanny had told her what a burden I was. Anner would leave her big, old bag down by the highway, where she got off the bus, and waddled up the hill to the house. She would then demand that I go retrieve it for her. Of course it weighed a ton, and I was probably six or seven, struggling to get the bag up the hill through the woods. Throughout her visit she yelled at me for anything and everything, and never a kind word came out of her mouth. Obviously, I couldn't wait for her to leave, and I am not sure Dad didn't feel the same way.

Nanny also had two brothers who migrated to Rossville, Georgia, which is close to Chattanooga. One was named Jessie and the other Floyd. Jessie was a drunk, smoked like a fire truck, and raised hell. Floyd was a preacher. A big event used to be when one of my uncles showed up in his car and took us all to Rossville to visit that part of the family. Even though I got to go, I always wound up with the worst seat in the vehicle and had to remain absolutely quiet for the entire trip. Tell a four-year-old to be quiet for a three-hour road trip! Ain't happening! So, of course, I was in trouble a lot on those trips. Jessie died of cancer while I was small, and Floyd died of old age sometime later.

I never remember my grandfather doing anything that made me feel wanted, either. He never talked to me, never asked me anything, never told me anything. Nothing! Even when I was very small, it was always like I was in his way, eating too much food, or taking up too much space. Try as I might, I only made it worse. If I tried to talk to him, I was annoying him. If I tried to help him do something, I was in the way. Nothing worked. One time when I was five or six, he took me fishing on one of the creeks close to our house. It was totally unlike him, and to this day, I don't know why he took me. I was so excited I could hardly stand it. The problem was that because I was so excited, I couldn't shut up. This gave him an excuse to never take me again.

My grandfather was a big man, probably 6'6" and weighed 250 or so. He was one of the strongest men I have ever known and could work most men into the ground. He had beautiful, wavy hair and cold blue eyes. He was a handsome man even in his old age. The pictures that I saw of him when he was younger looked like he was a real player.

He just had that look about him that said he was a ladies man, at least in his mind.

Like my grandmother, Dad was stubborn as the worst mule ever. He was a man of very few words. He hated the government, along with anyone in it. I remember one time a census worker came to the house, counting people, livestock, and so on. He asked Dad how many cows he had. He said, "Hold on a minute," and went back inside the house. He came back out moments later with his shotgun and told the guy to get the hell off his property and that it was none of his damn business how many cows he had.

Dad was a proud man and would never ask anyone for anything, nor expect anything from anyone. He seemed to have no emotions whatsoever. You could never tell what kind of mood he was in because he had only one mood, which was usually bad. I never saw him cry or laugh other than when we had company, and he wanted to put on a show.

Now strange as it may seem, considering his personality and meanness, my grandfather was a musician with some talent. He was an old-time fiddle player and played for many square dances around the area. He also played a banjo, although the fiddle was his primary instrument. He had a repertoire of some thirty or forty songs that he played totally by ear and memory. When the cousins or some pretty girls came around, he put on a real show for them. He had an old fiddle that belonged to one of my uncles. Its neck had broken off, and it had been repaired poorly. The story was that Uncle Jack, who also played the fiddle, was playing for a barn dance and got into a fight with some guy. He supposedly swung the fiddle at him and instead struck the hood of a car, breaking off the neck. At any rate, that fiddle still sounded great, and you could not tell it was broken unless you looked at it carefully.

I don't know if my grandfather actually loved the music or if he just played. I certainly couldn't tell from him. I do know I have a love for music and must have inherited it from him because my mother couldn't carry a tune in a tow sack.

Dad farmed the old-fashioned way, with a mule or horse and plow.

We had a wagon that was old and falling apart but got the job done. We farmed that forty-acre rock pile and actually turned out some meager crops. I learned to plow a horse when I was about seven years old. But I only did so on rare occasions because I could never do it the way Dad wanted it. My job was mostly to bring water out to him and the horse while he was plowing. Sometimes, he stopped to rest a few minutes while he drank and let me plow a couple of rows. Lucky for me, ole Charley was a gentle horse and had more sense about the job than I did. He was pretty tame and easy to handle and just sort of dragged me along with the plow. He responded to "gee" and "haw" and didn't require much else. I don't know what happened to Charley; he just disappeared one day. I never heard where he went or why. He was just gone.

Somehow Dad wound up with an old mule that was close to his match, personality wise. Dad was hooking up the plow to the singletree one day and trying to back the mule into it. The old mule suddenly went crazy and started kicking and braying like mad. When he was finally brought under control, he had torn the harness and plow all to hell. Well Dad was not the kind of person to take that from anything, especially a mule, so he went to the woodpile and picked up a slab of wood about the size of a two by four. He walked up to that old mule and hit him square between the eyes. The mule went down on his front knees and started shaking. It took a few minutes for him to recover and stagger to his feet. Dad immediately got in touch with someone with a cattle truck, who came and took the mule away. I don't know what happened to him, but he was gone from Whitehall. Dad didn't take kindly to anything that crossed him, especially an animal that didn't want to work. And he had absolutely no patience for pets.

My grandfather smoked a pipe constantly; I never remember him without it. He smoked one brand of tobacco, Country Gentleman. Country Gentleman was essentially pure, raw tobacco that had been cured and then cut into fine particles. You could smoke this stuff in either a pipe or roll it into a cigarette. The tobacco came in a little sack with drawstrings at the top. Rolling papers were conveniently tucked into the side of the sack. I started smoking at an early age and, of course, the tobacco of choice was Country Gentleman. By the time I was ten, I could roll a cigarette with one hand, just like the cowboys in the movies. Not much to brag about today, but at the time I thought it was hot stuff.

Dad had a terrible cough for as long as I can remember. I don't know if it was caused by the smoking or something else, but it was a deep cough, and he kept it even in the summer. Along with the coughing came a god-awful-looking phlegm that he spit everywhere, including onto the stove. In the winter he spit right onto the side of the heater. So the spit sizzled and burned. Really pleasant! My grandmother put old newspapers on the floor for him to spit onto, which added to the grossness. Of course when any of the relatives or cousins came, everything was cleaned up until they left, and he was a little more sanitary with the coughing. In later years, one of my uncles took him to see a doctor, but he only treated him for a cold and sent him home. Dad refused to quit smoking his pipe, so the cough continued. Many nights he woke up and coughed for hours. About the only thing that seemed to ease the cough was a stiff shot of corn liquor from the jug he kept under the bed. He drank his corn liquor straight from a jug, and he didn't just take a sip, he gulped it. He smoked incessantly, ate what he wanted and when he wanted it, seldom went to the doctor, and still lived to be eighty-eight years old. So much for good living!

One of his favorite meals was to take cornbread and crumble it up onto a plate, chop green onions up in it, and pour bacon grease over all of the mixture. It is just as well that he never went to doctors. If they had told him to stop doing something, it would have only made him do it more. He was just that stubborn.

CHAPTER 5

School

Starting first grade is always an interesting time in a young person's life. It's full of anticipation, excitement, and fear. Dread can usually be added to the mix as well. For me, it was even more traumatic than for most kids. For one thing, I had never used a flush toilet in my life. My mother really couldn't teach me because she didn't have any more experience with toilets than I did. I had also not been around other people that much. Back in those days, there was no such thing as kindergarten or preschool, and I started first grade my very first day of ever going to school. After much discussion, it was determined that whoever my teacher was, she would have to educate me on the finer points of flushing a toilet.

Fortunately, my first-grade teacher was Ms. Florence "Punt" Davenport. Ms. Davenport was a chubby, short, kindly lady, probably in her mid-fifties. She had been teaching at the same school forever. She was a jewel who took me under her wing and made sure that I survived. One of the most significant things I remember about Ms. Davenport was that she often shared her cookies with me during our midmorning break. I never had money to buy anything and just sat there, while most of the other kids munched away on potato chips or cookies. I guess she felt sorry for me not having any and would share hers. At any rate, it made a little country boy feel really special.

I also remember using those old workbooks that were made out of really cheap paper. They were used for all sorts of subjects, such as writing and math. And they tore easily if you made a mistake and had to erase.

While I was in first grade, some of the faculty, along with Ms. Davenport, began to notice I had difficulty hearing. They tried moving me to the front of the class, but I still had trouble. I don't know who was involved or how it happened, but someone arranged for me to go to the doctor for a checkup. The doctor told my mother I needed to have my tonsils taken out immediately, or I would lose all my hearing. The Parent and Teachers Association of Valley Head arranged for me to go to the hospital and have my tonsils removed. Someone in the group then paid the bill.

Going to the hospital was a big adventure, since I had never even been to a doctor at the time. I remember to this day being put to sleep for the surgery. Back then, ether was used as an anesthesia. The hospital staff put this big mask over my face and told me to breathe in normally. I remember feeling as though I was falling down a deep hole. I spiraled downward into blackness for what seemed like an eternity, never reaching bottom. Sometime later, I woke up and felt a large bump on my gums in front. I didn't have any front teeth on top when I went to the hospital, and the instrument used to keep my mouth open had slipped, bruising my gums. I thought I had suddenly grown a tooth in front. I got all excited but couldn't tell my mother because of the surgery.

The most exciting part of the ordeal was that when it was over, I got to eat all the ice cream I wanted. Even with the pain of the surgery, this was a good deal, as I had never eaten real, store-bought ice cream.

To this day, I don't know for sure who was responsible for making the surgery happen, but it probably saved my life. It certainly changed it. What is hard to believe is that my mother accepted the charity. That was totally unlike her, but I am certainly glad she did.

Getting to school was almost as traumatic as being in school. To get there I had to walk a half mile through Whitehall Cemetery and down to the main highway to wait for the bus. The bus would pick me up and then ramble around all over hell's half acre, picking up other kids. Some of the routes took two hours or more to complete before getting to the school ground. In the winter, it was especially difficult because those old buses did not have any heat. Because of the long route, most of us had to be at the stop early in the morning. Many days we were half frozen by the time we got to school.

There were many interesting things to see along the route to school. Strange people, different-looking houses, and yard decorations kept us entertained along the way. At one particular house way out in the middle of nowhere, there was a young boy, maybe ten or twelve years old, kept chained to the front porch of the house. Every time we passed the house, all the kids would rush to that side of the bus to gawk at this poor kid. This child always had a wild look about him, and there were all sorts of stories about why he was there. I am sure the truth was probably never known, but the best story was that his mother had him when she was real young and left him with his grandmother to raise. She was elderly and could not keep up with him, so in desperation, she chained him to the porch. I feel really bad today because at the time, all of us in one way or the other made fun of this unfortunate child, regardless of what the circumstances were.

First grade was easy for me because I had already learned so much from my mother. When the end of the school year came, I was promoted to second grade. However, when the next school year started, I was moved up to the third grade. Someone walked into the second-grade classroom and told me to come with her. When we got to the third-grade classroom, I was told to sit by this little girl toward the front of the class. Well, I guess I thought that "Sit next to her" meant just that. So I picked up my desk and moved it right beside her, close enough to touch. Of course that was not what the teacher meant. The little girl was embarrassed, and so was I. What a way to start the year. The girl's name was Brenda, and she turned out to be a really sweet girl.

The third grade was my favorite year of all, even with the unfortunate beginning. Ms. Willie Lee Webster was our teacher, and she was another special woman. She had purple hair and wore purple glasses. Aside from her somewhat quirky appearance, she was a no-nonsense woman who kept a big old paddle in her desk and would use it in a heartbeat. One day some kid in the class was acting up, so she got her paddle, and as she was applying some "attention getting" to his rear end, the paddle broke. A big piece of it flew up in the air and landed in our fish tank, making a big splash. The whole class started laughing, and so did Ms. Webster. She was laughing so hard that she couldn't finish the paddling. So the kid was spared and lived to act up another day.

Our little country school was always putting on a play or hosting some sort of show. One time there was a magic show in the main auditorium that cost a dime to see. Of course I didn't have a dime and wound up being the only kid left in the classroom, while everyone else went to the show. I was sitting there by myself when Ms. Webster came back and got me. She gave me a dime, and I got to see the show like everyone else. Once again I was made to feel special.

While I was in third grade, a boy in the class brought a book to school and let me look at it. It was a great, big book about Roy Rogers. Now Roy Rogers was a huge television and movie star at the time, but I had never heard of him. I wound up reading the entire book and later managed to get my own copy. I became obsessed with Roy Rogers. I somehow got a pistol set from somewhere and a hat. I tried to look and act just like this western hero. I wanted a horse in the worst way, so I decided one day to write Roy Rogers and ask him for one. Surely he would see the need and send me one, since he had lots of them on his ranch. After all, it said so in the book. So I wrote him a letter asking for a horse and mailed it to Roy Rogers, Hollywood, California. I never got an answer—or a horse—and for a long time felt cheated. But at least I tried.

I went to that same little country school until the ninth grade. By that time, my mother had moved to town to be closer to her job at the laundry, and it was time for a change. I was teased unmercifully all through elementary school. A lot of the teasing was my own fault, I suppose, as I was always saying things to get attention. The worst teasing was about my nickname, which was Pedro. Now the Spanish pronunciation would be "Paydro," but these ignorant country kids called me Peedro, which made it even worse. How I got this nickname was my own fault. It started when I found an old booklet in somebody's trunk one day. It was a language introduction manual for the Fiji Islands. The book had been brought home by one of my uncles, who had been stationed there during World War II. After reading the booklet, I concocted the notion that I could speak the language. It was a great story, and one sure to get attention. So every morning when I got on the bus, I used some of the words from the booklet, along with some I made up. Soon older kids started goading me to talk "Fijian" for them. What I didn't realize at the time was that they were making fun of me and using me for entertainment. These kids apparently didn't know where Fiji was or that it was not Spanish because they started calling me Pedro when they got me to "talk" for them. The name stuck like cheap glue for the rest of the time I went to school there. The harder I fought, the more the teasing came, and I hated every minute of it. I was obsessed with that nickname and dreamed of the day I could leave and never hear it again. So when the chance came to switch schools, I jumped at it. I have never been as relieved as I was to walk into a new school and have people call me by my name. No more Pedro! Just to make sure, I started using my first name instead of what my mother had called me for years. I didn't want to take any chances of Pedro slipping up again.

I was never really good at any sport except baseball. I loved the game and was actually pretty good for never having any formal training or coaching. I would spend hours throwing a ball up in the air and catching it or bouncing it off the front part of the house. That really infuriated Nanny, and she would yell at me to stop. But I usually kept on or moved to another part of the house. I soon learned how to catch pretty well. Somehow my mother got me a really cheap glove from Western Auto. It was a pitiful glove, but to me, it was the greatest thing on earth. I had my own glove! When I was about eleven or twelve, the school formed a Little League team for the summer. One of my friends who lived close by signed up, and his mother had a car. He agreed to let me ride to practice and games with him, so I signed up, too.

The coach was Earl Warren. He was also one of the head coaches for the school and doing this as a volunteer. He was a great coach, and

I learned a lot about the game and about life from him. He was a kind man but all business. I played outfield and could catch almost anything that came my way, even with my old, cheap glove.

In the very first game I ever played in, I hit a home run with runners on base. It was actually a triple that turned into a home run when the outfielder bobbled the ball and was late getting it back in. I rounded third, and the third base coach waved me on through. I saw the catcher preparing to catch the ball, so I slid into him hard. He dropped the ball, making me safe at home. He was shaken up pretty bad from the collision, and I went over to him to apologize for hurting him. The coach and other players started yelling at me to forget about him as we just went ahead in the score. So much for humanity!

Baseball was going really well, until someone decided we should get uniforms and look like a real team. One of the local businesses offered to sponsor us, which would ease the cost a bit, but it was still out of my reach. So I had no uniform. One day at practice, Coach Warren called me over and told me that he was going to buy my uniform for me out of his pocket. He said, "I understand that you don't have a daddy, so I am going to take care of your uniform." I was ecstatic, until I got home and told my mother. She was having none of that and told me I could not go back to baseball ever again. She would rather have me quit than swallow her pride and allow someone to do something nice for me. I never went back.

One day after school started back, Coach Warren asked me why I quit the team. I told the worst lie of my life when I said that it was just too hot to play baseball. He replied, "Yeah for girls." I lost all his respect that day and was never close to him again. I think back today and wonder what might have been different if I could have stayed. I really believe that with the right coaching, I could have gone quite far in baseball. I was really pretty good.

CHAPTER 6

Christmas at Whitehall

I guess the one good thing about growing up poor is that you don't expect a lot, and when something good does come along, you really appreciate it. This is especially true at Christmastime. There were years when I was small that I got very little for Christmas. But because I had never had very much, it was barely noticed. I remember one year I got a large rubber ball wrapped up in tissue paper. Of course, I got this along with a couple of oranges and some candy I found hanging in my stocking. I was as happy with that ball as I would have been with a new bicycle.

Back then, the Christmas tree was usually decorated with colored balls and strings of popcorn because we didn't have electricity for lights. Mother managed to get some tinsel one year and covered the tree with it. Of course when Christmas was over, she took the tinsel down and saved it for the next year. Most Christmases my grandmother would make homemade peanut brittle. We grew peanuts on the farm, and they were ready for harvest just before Christmas. She would make a huge piece of brittle and then break it into small pieces. A good portion of the brittle was mailed to one or more of my uncles, who were serving in the military somewhere. But my brother and I devoured the rest.

One particular year I remember being at the grocery store with my mother when she was shopping for Christmas dinner. She had placed several items in her buggy and was going through the checkout line when the cashier told her how much she owed. She didn't have enough money to pay for everything and had to put some items back. One of the items was a jar of mincemeat pie filling. It killed her pride to have to do that, especially in front of a store full of people. She never asked for anything. She just placed it back on the shelf and paid for what she could and left. As soon as I had the means, I started buying a jar of mincemeat every year at Christmas and giving it away. It is a small token and may not mean much to anyone else, but it is special to me.

After Mother went to work at the laundry, things got a little better, and Christmas became a bigger deal. But even with some money coming in, she still didn't go overboard. She would save all year long just to buy one special gift for me. She usually supplemented that with a couple of more practical gifts, like gloves or a new hat and maybe a new book or two.

The other thing about being poor was that when I did get something special, I tended to take care of it and make it last. There were a few gifts that really stood out and made me feel like the luckiest kid alive. One year I got a real telegraph set that could send and receive Morse code. It ran on batteries, so I didn't have to worry about electricity. The only problem was that I was the only one who knew any of the code. I still managed to have a great time with it in spite of the fact no one could talk to me.

Probably the most special gift that I ever received was a portable radio. I have always loved music, and the thought of being able to tune in at any time was beyond my wildest dreams. Battery radios back then were much different than those we have today. They used a huge battery called a dry cell, which was bigger than a car battery. These batteries only lasted a few hours, so play time was rationed. We actually had a big radio off and on while I was growing up, but my granddaddy usually chose what we listened to, and very rarely was it music. I didn't ask for a radio for Christmas because I never really asked for anything. My mother got it for me totally on her own. This radio used a much smaller dry cell than the big console models that most people owned. For once I could listen to exactly what I wanted to and when I wanted to. I would carry it out into the orchard and sit in an apple tree, listening to music and eating green apples. It didn't get much better than that. I have no idea what the radio cost or how many weeks Mother had to save to get it, but it sure made a little kid happy on Christmas morning. I still have the radio. Of course you can't buy those dry cell batteries anymore, but if I could, the radio would work just like when it was new.

These special Christmases made it so much easier to go back to school from Christmas break. The teachers made a point of asking the kids to stand and tell all the things they got for Christmas. It hurt when all you got was a rubber ball and some candy. But when you got a radio, you couldn't wait for it to be your turn.

The little school I attended always decorated for Christmas, and most teachers decorated trees for their classrooms. A couple of classroom trees had lights that bubbled, and I was always mesmerized by them. Several teachers bought gifts for each student out of their own pockets and put the gifts under the tree just before we got out of school for the holiday. I remember that Ms. Davenport and Ms. Webster both got me a Little Golden Book. Ms. Davenport bought me one about a little girl and the circus, and Ms. Webster got me one about a little fat policeman. I wonder if that book had anything to do with my future career.

When I was about seven or eight years old, I received a gift from my uncle Jack that was very special, even though it wasn't for Christmas. He was home on leave from the military and for some reason decided to go into Fort Payne and buy me a great big tricycle. He also bought my brother a full-size bicycle, complete with bag rack, horn, and light. This tricycle was not your typical trike. It was huge and had a chain-drive mechanism similar to a bicycle's. The only difference was that the tricycle didn't have any brakes. I thought that tricycle was the most amazing thing I had ever seen, and I rode it everywhere.

One day my brother wasn't satisfied with riding his new bicycle and decided he would take my tricycle. Of course he never asked. He just took it and rode it down the cemetery hill. He quickly got into big trouble when he forgot, or didn't bother to check, the fact that the trike didn't have brakes. About halfway down the hill, he lost control of the trike and wound up riding about fifty feet or so down the barbed wire fence that ran along the road. He was cut up pretty badly. When he came limping back to the house dragging the tricycle, Nanny had to patch him up and stop the considerable bleeding. Of course he never went to the doctor, and ever since, he has had terrible scars across his body. Many years later, after he left for the navy, I sort of inherited the bicycle and managed to keep it going for several more years. I became very adept at bicycle mechanics and could fix almost anything.

CHAPTER 7

The Kids of Whitehall

Growing up in rural Alabama was full of adventure. In spite of all the hardships, I had a lot of fun. Living so far back in the woods meant that there were not a lot of other folks around and even fewer kids close to my age. Right after I started school, I came to realize there was another kid my age who lived about a mile through the woods from my house. All this time I thought we were the only people around. Who knew? Larry and I became close friends and remained so for years. He was able to look past the fact that I was so much worse off than he was and that I didn't have a lot of the things he took for granted. Larry and I spent many hours together, hiking around in the woods. Sometimes we went down to one of the many creeks that ran through the valley, and on occasion we went camping and fishing.

Over the years we came up with all sorts of role-playing activities. For a long time we were Ace and Spade. Larry was Ace, and I was Spade. We made up all sorts of scenes that we played out as we went through the woods. We stayed in character the entire time we were gone. Another role-playing act was Jed and Clem. Larry was Jed, and I was Clem. These characters were somewhat like "Snuffy Smith," which, as I look back, probably didn't require all that much acting.

I went with Larry to a public swimming pool for the first time in my life. I don't ever remember learning to swim; it seems I just always knew how. I learned by watching the other guys and then just doing it.

You either swam or were left out, so I swam. We spent many summer days swimming in the creeks and ponds around our houses.

Not everything that we got into ended well, and there were times it was evident God was looking out for us. One time in particular, we were hitting rocks out in the yard with a slab of lumber. I pitched a rock to Larry, and he hit a line drive right back to my face. The rock struck me right in the corner of my eye and nose, missing my eye by a fraction of an inch. The blow knocked me flat on my back and out cold for several minutes. It crushed the sinus passages in my nose but did not affect my vision. My treatment was cold towels held over my eye to reduce the swelling.

Another time Larry and I were looking for something exciting to do with our time and decided that it would be great fun to stick a shotgun shell down into the handlebar of an old bicycle that was rusting in the backyard and shoot it with a BB gun. The shell fit nicely, and we thought this would make a great explosion, probably blowing up the handlebar as well. Larry backed off about twenty yards or so and shot at the shell several times, until he finally hit it. The shell went off with a loud explosion, just as we planned. But what we didn't plan was the cap of the shotgun shell flying back and hitting Larry right between the eyes. The cap is a small brass cup that holds a powder charge and when struck, explodes and lights off the powder in the shell. When the shell went off, the cap was blown out of the casing, and it stuck square in the middle of Larry's head. In both cases, if we had moved one inch or if the projectile had struck just a hair off, we would have been blinded.

When I was about eleven or twelve, Uncle Jack had electricity run to the old house. He also put a deep pump in the well and had water run to the house. All of a sudden, we were this modern family. The first thing that my grandfather did was go around the house, putting tape over the outlets. When somebody asked him why, he replied, "To keep the electricity from getting out and wasting."

Nanny bought an old school bus body and had it delivered up to the house to be used for storage. This was a common practice back then, and these old bus bodies made great out buildings. We kept all sorts of junk in there, and it was a great place to go just to get away from everybody now and then. I decided it would be even better if it had electricity, like the house, and got down the old *Funk and Wagnalls*. I found some old antenna wire, which was barely good enough for TV signals, and attached a plug on one end and a socket on the other. I plugged it into a wall outlet and presto, I had electricity in the bus. How I kept from electrocuting myself is a miracle. Having light in the bus meant that Larry and I could go out there at night and play Monopoly or whatever. We had many all-night games in that old bus.

One time we decided it would be even better if we had something to drink. Now none of us had ever had alcohol of any kind before, and we had no idea what the effects might be. It just seemed like a good idea at the time. Nanny kept a big jug of Mogen David wine beside her bed, just like Dad kept his 'shine. She would take a shot every now and then for medicinal purposes, I am sure. This particular wine is called Mad Dog on the streets and is god awful, but we wanted to try it anyway, so I decided to slip some of hers out to the bus. The jug was right beside her side of the bed, which was right by the window. I came up with this brilliant plan to siphon the wine from the jug into a jar and then take the jar to the bus. We slipped up to the house and eased the window open, and I reached in and opened the jug. I slipped a short, rubber tube down into the jug and siphoned. The wine started running, and all was good. About halfway through this operation, Larry asked me, "Why don't you just take the jug out of the window, pour out what we need, and then put the jug back?" Hmmm! That would make sense but then it wouldn't be a great heist like this. So I finished with the siphon task, and as soon as we had enough wine, I slipped back to the bus, and we started the game. Well it only took a couple of glasses of the wine, and we were wasted. We were laughing and falling all over the bus. It was a wonder that we didn't wake everybody with all the noise. We woke up the next morning after passing out in the bus and, of course, we had a terrible headache. That was the last time I ever thought about sneaking any kind of alcohol from either of them.

There were numerous other children within a few miles of my house with whom I grew up and roamed the ridges. George, Patsy,

Jean, Johnny, and Mike were all a part of growing up and still hold special places in my heart. George and Patsy were brother and sister, and Jean was their cousin. I later had a serious crush on Jean, but we never dated. We did double date once, however, but fate or whatever kept us from ever dating each other. I was sad to learn much later that Jean had passed away. She apparently died in her sleep, with no explanation.

George was in many ways just like me, which was probably what led to our friendship. George was the son of a single mother and also lived with his grandfather and grandmother. The difference was that he actually had a father, just not one who was in his life. Another big difference was that his grandmother and grandfather were the exact opposite of my grandparents. George's grandmother and "Uncle Jim" were saintly old folks. I spent many nights at their house, sharing what little food they had, and they never once made me feel less than welcome. His grandfather talked to me just like he did George and dispensed sage-old wisdom about life as if I were a member of the family. He even took George and me squirrel hunting a couple of times. It was obvious that both grandparents loved George and Patsy, and they were not afraid or ashamed to show it. I never once heard either grandparent raise his or her voice at anyone or talk bad about anyone. They were just good people.

George's mother, on the other hand, was somewhat like my own mother. She was stubborn and set in her ways, with very little patience for anyone. However, she never made me feel unwelcome or that I was in the way.

I ate many meals at their house, and they were always the same thing. Breakfast was always hard fried eggs and biscuits, and supper was beans and taters with cornbread. The beans were dried pintos that were boiled with a small piece of pork fatback for seasoning. The potatoes were boiled into mush with no seasoning at all. Pintos were a staple back then because they could be stored forever without refrigeration and provided ample protein and starch. On rare occasions, Sunday dinner was fried chicken to go along with the beans and potatoes. I loved to go there and always loved mealtime, regardless of what they were having.

When I was about ten years old, I came up with the idea of forming a club that I called the Zorro Brothers. I do not know where the idea came from, but it was pretty elaborate, if I do say so myself. I knew who Zorro was from a comic book, and that seemed like a great name for a club to me. I came up with a secret code, a sign, and rules of conduct for the members to live by. Once all the basics were covered, I began recruiting members. For some reason, George didn't think he wanted to join my august group, so I thought I would send him a letter to encourage him. The letter was actually pretty threatening and said all sorts of bad things would happen to him if he didn't join. It basically said, "If you ain't with us, you are the enemy, and you will rue the day." I sent this letter to his house, and his mother intercepted it. She was not amused and did not see the humor in it. To say the least, she took it seriously and stopped me from coming to their house for a long time.

The Zorro Brothers were short lived. We eventually went on to other entertainment pursuits. We spent hours and hours playing cowboys and Indians or roaming around in the woods between his house and mine. A beautiful creek ran right in front of his house, and one had to cross the creek on a narrow bridge or on a foot log to get to the road. This is the same foot log that I jumped off and stuck the nail through my foot.

Johnny was actually a second cousin of mine, whom I discovered in about the fourth grade. He lived about five miles from me, way out in the country, with his mother, Aunt Maggie and daddy, Calvin. I also spent many nights and weekends at Johnny's house, and Aunt Maggie was as good as they come. Aunt Maggie was really my mother's first cousin on my grandfather's side, but in Alabama, anybody can be an aunt. I could go to her house at any time of the day or night and always be welcome. She was a very quiet person with a deep Southern drawl, who basically allowed us to do most anything we wanted.

Calvin, on the other hand, was a real piece of work. He was a little more outgoing than Aunt Maggie and was great fun to be around. Calvin had a reputation as a corn liquor maker and was on probation off and on the entire time that I knew him. The funny thing about bootleggers is that many times their best customers are the same ones who put them in jail. Judges, lawyers, and the sheriff always seem to like good corn whiskey and will pay well for it. The problem comes when some deacon or teetotaler gets wind of the whiskey-making operation and puts pressure on law enforcement to shut it down. There is going to be a raid, and the liquor maker gets stuck. I am sure this happened to Calvin on more than one occasion.

Calvin had a dry sense of humor and was always cracking us up. He was a gentle soul, and I never heard him speak ill of anyone or try to harm anyone. He just liked to make and drink corn whiskey. From what I knew about him, he was pretty good at both.

Johnny and I spent many days together fishing, camping, and swimming in the creek that ran in front of their house. The same creek ran by their house and George's, just a few miles apart. After a couple of years, the person who owned the house where Johnny lived decided to dam up the creek a little ways from the house and make a lake. This project involved blasting rock from a huge hillside and then piling the rock on the creek, forming a dam across it. These were exciting times for Johnny and me. We watched for hours as the workmen drilled deep holes into the rock wall. When the workday was finished, we went up onto the hill and played. There were always all sorts of interesting equipment and parts left up there to explore and mess with.

When enough holes had been drilled to blast, the real excitement began. Dynamite was brought in and carefully placed into the holes down the side of the hill. Fuses were run to connect the sticks to a central blasting switch. And then it was time to blow. The foreman came down and warned all that blasting was about to begin and encouraged us to take cover. Johnny and I were having none of that take cover stuff because we wanted to see everything as it happened. The blasting crew sounded a siren as a last warning and then yelled, "Fire in the hole!" Boom! Down came tons of rock and gravel.

The blast sent large rocks way into the air, and who knew where they would come down? But that didn't stop us from being out in the open. Most of the blasts were fairly surgical, and very little went flying off course. But on occasion, it got pretty wild. One time we even climbed a tall pine tree to get an even better look. While we were up there, a rattlesnake decided it liked the shade of the same tree to take a nap. When we started back down, we woke it up, and the snake was not happy. We stayed up there for a little while, trying to figure out how to get out of this mess. When no good idea came to us, we decided to just go for it. We came down out of the tree and jumped right on top of the snake, running like mad. The snake was probably scared worse than we were, and we were lucky to escape without serious injury.

Once the dam started taking shape and the water started backing up, the lake became our new swimming hole. At first, the water was only a couple of feet deep, but as time went on, it got deeper and deeper, reaching a depth of eight feet or so. Thinking back, I don't remember if I learned to swim in this lake or the public swimming pool. It could have been either place because as I mentioned before, I don't remember learning to swim at all.

Johnny had a fascination with comic books and had quite a collection. We spent hours at night, lying in bed reading his stack of books. Eventually Aunt Maggie came in and made us turn off the light. Of course, if it had not been for Johnny, I would never have seen a comic book, as we certainly could not afford them.

The woods around us were full of good things to eat. You just had to know where to look and what to look for. We would be out tramping around, and a blackberry or blueberry patch would provide a great snack while we were out. Wild strawberries, gooseberries, and wild grapes were everywhere, there for the taking. Once when we were out, we stumbled upon a honey tree, full of bees and honey. We decided we just had to have some of the honey and set about a plan to get rid of the bees. We found some old rags and stuffed them into a hole at the base of the tree. We lit the rags and waited for the bees to leave. Bees don't like smoke, and those that stay around are tranquilized to the point that they won't sting you. Our plan would have been great except for the fact the rags wouldn't burn. We poked around at them but could not get them going. So we abandoned the plan and went about finding another adventure somewhere else. Unfortunately, the rags did light right after we left. They caught the tree on fire and burned it to the ground, along with about fifty acres of timberland. All that and we still didn't get any honey!

One really amazing thing about these particular years was that I carried a gun everywhere I went. Keep in mind I was around ten or so, roaming around in the woods by myself, carrying a loaded gun. If you did that today, your parents would be arrested. Back then, folks thought nothing of it; it was as natural as eating or sleeping. I had a gun for as far back as I can remember. How I got the gun is unusual because I basically built it from parts. I found the gun while prowling around in Dad's old trunk. It was a little twenty-two rifle and was in about twenty parts. The gun was a giveaway for a salve company that rewarded young boys for selling their product. You could earn a bicycle, rifle, tent, or other neat things just for selling this stuff. Well someone apparently earned this little gun at some point, and Dad somehow wound up with it. Unfortunately, it was broken and in total disarray. I asked him for the gun one day, and to my surprise, he gave it to me. I think he believed that I couldn't fix it and would bring it back. But he was wrong. I was not going to let a little mechanical difficulty stop me if it meant that I would have my own gun. So I got all the parts and figured out where they went and what they did. The real problem was that the gun was really cheaply made and was spot welded. The weld had broken, and that caused all the problems. I couldn't get it rewelded, of course, so I did the next best thing. I taped it together with an old roll of electrical tape that I found somewhere. And lo and behold, it worked like new.

My next project was to learn to shoot it. Ammunition wasn't cheap, so I needed to hit what I was aiming at. I got the old *Funk and Wagnalls* down and learned the basics of marksmanship. I taught myself the finer points of shooting and became quite a good shot. I could shoot the bottom out of a Coke bottle through the top from about twenty five yards away. And I could cut a string with a rock hanging on it from about the same distance. Birds, squirrels, rabbits, and other small game were no match for that little gun.

Several years later, some slick cousin of Dad's paid us a visit and convinced Dad he could get it repaired and back to its original condition. He took my little gun away, and it was never seen again. I was heartbroken, of course, but there was nothing I could do about it. I replaced the twenty-two with an old, beat-up shotgun that I traded for, but it was never the same as the little rifle. Johnny had guns around and occasionally went hunting with me, but he didn't have the same interest in them that I did.

Johnny was quite a mechanic and was always tinkering with something. He found an old Whizzer motorbike somewhere that was missing the motor. He also found an old washing machine that used a gasoline engine to operate the agitator and wringer. The little motor was maybe two or three horsepower and cranked with a foot starter, similar to those found on large motorcycles. Johnny put the motor from the washing machine on the bike, and after some tinkering, got it running. Just like that he had a gas-powered bike. Johnny followed up on his mechanical ability with trade school, and after being drafted into the army, became a highly sought after Porsche mechanic.

Many years later, after Johnny and I had both left home, Aunt Maggie lived in the same house that I was born in. I went to see her one time and got to see the little house. Of course, I had no memories of ever being there, but it was still interesting to know that I had arrived on the earth in that same house years earlier.

Mike lived a couple of miles from me, down a long dirt road that seemed to go into nowhere. His house was at the very end of the road. He moved there when I was about eight or so, as best as I can remember. Mike lived there with his father and mother, another two "saintly" persons. There was a laying-hen operation on the property, and his dad managed it. There were three huge chicken houses, all crammed with layers. The eggs were gathered, graded, packaged, and shipped to a buyer. One of my first paying jobs was gathering eggs for his dad. He paid me fifty cents to help Mike in the evenings pick up the thousands of eggs the chickens laid each day. It was hard work, but to me, fifty cents was a small fortune. Mike and I spent a lot of time together, and I ate many meals at his house, especially on nights when his mother fixed fish sticks. I thought I had died and gone to heaven the first time I ate them.

Laying houses tend to attract great big rats because they come into the houses to eat the chicken feed. Every so often, we would have a "rat killing," which is one of the wildest times that I have ever had. A successful rat killing has to be done at night because that's when they come out and feed. We all met up at Mikes with guns and rat shot. No shotguns or regular bullets could be used. They were too dangerous and would kill more chickens than rats. Rat shot is a twenty-two cartridge filled with tiny pellets, similar to a shotgun shell. From a distance, they would not harm the chickens but were deadly on the rats. We waited patiently until about nine or ten o'clock and then slipped down to one of the houses, easing the door open slightly. Mike flipped on the main light switch, and all hell broke loose. Rats scattered everywhere, running at breakneck speed down the tops of the chicken cages and occasionally jumping off and scurrying across the floor of the house. We followed in hot pursuit, blazing away with the twenty-twos. Rats, and occasionally, chickens were falling dead everywhere. After about an hour of this, we collected our kill, which went immediately into the big dump out back, and headed for home. Dead chickens, rats, and all went into a big burn pit behind the laying houses, where at some point Mike's dad would pour fuel on the pile and burn it. Sometimes I spent the night, and at other times, I had to walk the two miles or so home in the dark. But I did carry a gun, so it wasn't too bad. One big problem with rat killings is that it is hard to shoot when you are laughing so hard you wet your pants.

Mike had an older sister. Her husband was somewhat of a professional student because he was always going to college somewhere. He was a little on the strange side but was a lot of fun to be around. One time when I was about twelve or thirteen, he happened to be visiting and decided that we should go into Talley Cave, which is close to Valley Head. I had heard stories about this cave for years from kids at school. Some even claimed to have gone into the cave and regaled us with stories of a lake with blind fish and a bottomless pit deep in the cave. The rumor was that this particular cave went all the way through Lookout Mountain and came out over in Georgia somewhere. Indians supposedly used this cave for many years as a meeting place, and stories of criminals using it as a hideout were plentiful. Larry and I were visiting Mike and went along to the cave. None of us had ever been inside a cave, and we certainly didn't have any equipment for such an adventure. Mike's brother-in-law had one flashlight, and that was the extent of the equipment we had. We pressed on, however, and soon found the entrance to the cave, which was a small hole in the side of Lookout Mountain.

To get into the cave, we had to crawl on our stomachs about fifty yards or so. It was pitch-black and really creepy. Things fluttered around just over our heads, but we couldn't see what they were. I assume that they were bats, but who knows? After crawling the length of the tunnel, we came out into a huge room. There was a fire pit that someone had built in the center of the room, and there was a supply of firewood stacked close by. Corridors went off in several directions from the main room. We decided to build a fire in the pit and use that as our reference point to get back.

After getting the fire going, we decided on a path and started off. There were stalactites and stalagmites everywhere, and water dripped constantly. Every sound echoed though the cave, and drips of water became the sound of wild creatures moving around if you let your mind wander. We had to be careful where we stepped because we didn't know if a puddle was really a puddle or some deep chasm that we could fall into and never be found. We had to walk holding onto each other because only the lead person had a light. The rest of us were in total darkness except right in front. Several times we had to slide down an embankment of several feet. Most of the time, you could see what lay below you, but the real concern was how we were going to get back up with no rope or other gear.

After trekking through what seemed like miles of passageways and tunnels, we found the so-called bottomless pit. We actually stumbled onto it, and we were lucky we didn't fall into it. I don't know for sure if it was, in fact, bottomless, but we chunked several big rocks into it and never heard them hit bottom. You could not see the bottom with our flashlight, so it was pretty deep. We carefully found our way around the hole and moved on through the cave.

After another several minutes we came upon a large body of

water. I don't know how big it was because we could not see across it with our light. I don't know how deep it was because no one was willing to wade in to find out. We didn't see any fish in the water, so I don't know if they were blind or not. We decided it was time to head back to the opening and out of the cave.

We stumbled around for quite a while, just going in whatever direction felt right. Sometimes we could see the light flickering, and sometimes we couldn't, which added to the absolute insanity of the adventure. The flashlight we had was getting dimmer and dimmer, and if it went out, we would be in big trouble. We would have been lost in the cave forever because no one knew we were in there. We didn't bother to notify anyone before we went in. At some point on our way back, Mike's brother-in-law thought he saw something moving around and pulled out a pistol and started shooting. Bullets bounced off the walls, and the sound was deafening. We yelled for him to stop shooting and to calm down. Just think, this is the adult in the group! We were lucky that the gunfire didn't cause a cave-in. We finally made it back to the entrance and scooted out through the tunnel. When we finally made it out, we realized that we had been inside the cave for over four hours. We had lived through the adventure of a lifetime.

Two of the wildest kids I grew up with had to be James and Terry. James was the older of the two and was maybe a year older than I. Terry was a few years younger than all of us. I met these two when I was maybe ten years old. They moved to Whitehall from somewhere around Chattanooga and had rented this big farm up the road from us. Their daddy drove a milk truck for a big dairy and traveled back and forth from Rossville, Georgia, a couple times a week.

The first time I was ever at their house was with my mother. I don't know how she knew about them, but we walked up to their house one Saturday. While the grown-ups were having coffee, the boys and I ran off to get into some mischief. They immediately started competing for my attention, like they had never been around anyone before. Each was trying to outdo the other and give me everything they owned. One tried to give me a coat, and the other tried to give me a special drinking cup. I really didn't want them to give me anything; I just wanted them to like me.

We hit it off pretty well once the gift giving was past us. We arranged for me to spend the night with them a few nights later, and thus began a long-term friendship that had many adventures attached. These were outdoor kids just like me, and together we spent many nights camping out or going swimming down in the creek that ran several hundred feet behind the house.

Their daddy intended to farm the land and raise cattle and horses. I think his plan was to get the boys as far away from the city as possible, and that farm was it. He expected the boys to work and was pretty demanding about doing so. The truth is, it was a pretty good life. The problem was that these kids were reckless and did things that even for me were a little out there. Things like shooting each other with BB guns or getting into a corn cob fight. They were always daring each other to do stuff and would usually do it.

Like I said, this was a big farm with plenty of room to roam around in, and the creek ran right through the middle of it. We soon found a fairly deep swimming hole and crafted swings out over the water. The dare was who could do the craziest things off the swing. How we kept from drowning is a miracle.

The real fun began one day when their dad found a way to get the boys some horses. The Lookout Mountain area has long been known for its numerous summer camps. The camps run all summer long and shut down in the winter months. Some of the camps maintained a stable of horses for the kids to ride during camp season and then lent them out to people in the off season. All you had to do was feed and care for it, and it was yours until the next season.

Two horses were borrowed from one of the camps, and they soon showed up: a real tall and lanky roan gelding named Baldy and a small roan mare whose name I cannot remember. James took the old gelding, and Terry took the mare. The horses came complete with all the necessary tack, such as a saddle and bridle. These were fairly gentle horses; they had to be to survive in a summer camp. Their dad also devised a plan to get free help with the farmwork. If we wanted to ride, we had to work. Whatever farm work needed to be done, we did it. We gathered corn, harvested garden vegetables, and helped plow the fields. When the work was done, we got to ride the horses. On weekends there might be three or four extra kids around.

Probably the biggest job that we did was shucking corn for animal feed. After the corn was harvested from the field, it was brought up to the barn and the ears pulled from the cornstalks. The stalks were kept for fodder. The ears were fed into a machine that separated the grains of corn from the cob. Most of the time the work erupted into a huge corncob fight between the kids who were supposed to be working. How we kept from seriously injuring each other I have no idea, but we did. Eventually the work would get done, and it would be riding time.

We would saddle up the two camp horses, and off we went. If there were only four of us, we rode double. And if there were more, we took turns. The little mare was fast and fun to ride. But Baldy was either lazy or mentally deficient because, we could rarely persuade him to get beyond a canter. For the couple of summers the camp loaned them, we rode the horses everywhere. Almost every weekend, some of us would be at the farm, riding.

One of the biggest wrecks of my life occurred while riding with James and Terry. I have been in bicycle wrecks, car wrecks, and almost every other kind of disaster you can name but have never had a worse experience than this. Four of us were off riding one afternoon. I was riding double behind Terry on the mare, and someone else was riding behind James on Baldy. One of us decided it would be cool to race the horses, and away we went at a full gallop. The mare was way ahead of the other horse, when suddenly, the cinch that holds the saddle on either broke or came loose. As the saddle slowly slid sideways and off the horse, so did Terry and I. We fell off the horse onto the gravel road, and each of us bounced several times as we hit the ground. To add to the pain of the situation, the mare stepped on me as she ran past us. I had skin torn from every part of my body. The wind was knocked out of me, and I thought for several minutes that my back was broken. Of course, the horse kept running, leaving us lying there, thinking we were dead. When I was able to catch my breath, I got up and limped off to my house. Nanny got out a bottle of Mercurochrome and dabbed it all over my body, fussing every minute like I was interrupting something. Once again, I never went to the doctor.

James and Terry were driving a car before most people learned to ride a bicycle. The family had a big, old Oldsmobile that both of the boys drove everywhere. The family also had an older model Case tractor that they used to farm. Of course, both boys drove the tractor as well. One day they could not get the tractor started, and someone came up with the brilliant idea that we should pull the tractor with the Oldsmobile and start it that way. We hooked a chain to the front end of the tractor and then to the bumper of the Olds. Terry drove the tractor, and James fired up the Olds and pulled out on to the main highway. For some reason, we thought it would be smart if Larry and I rode on the top of the trunk, hanging on by our fingernails. I suppose it was to watch the chain or something, but who knows? At any rate, we were headed down the highway when James decided we were not going fast enough to start the tractor. He took the Olds up to over forty miles an hour. Now the tractor had a tricycle front end, which meant that the two wheels are very close together, making it difficult to control at slow speeds, much less forty miles per hour. Terry struggled to keep the tractor on the road, Larry and I were barely hanging on, and James was oblivious to any danger. Terry yelled to slow down, and Larry and I banged on the trunk, trying to get James to pull over. After all this, we never did get the tractor started. This whole episode is proof positive that God looks after fools and little children because if he hadn't, we surely would have killed ourselves that day.

James and Terry lived there until I was in the seventh grade and then moved back to Rossville or somewhere. We had many adventures and close calls, but the wildest accident happened one day when I was not there. As I heard the story, James and Terry were out in the field plowing. and As usual, they started acting the fool, and Terry fell off the tractor. James couldn't turn in time, and ran over Terry with the tractor. The accident messed Terry up pretty bad, causing severe internal injuries and a crushed pelvis. Terry lived, however, and continued as if nothing had happened.

I lost touch with both boys until many years later, after I had gone into the navy. I tracked them to Rossville and saw both James and Terry. James had gotten married, and Terry was as wild as ever.

CHAPTER 8

Cicero and Gladys

One of the more colorful characters I knew while growing up was Cicero. When I first met him, Cicero ran a small country store way out in the country where he sold mostly dry goods, canned goods, and other nonperishables. His first store was actually in an old house right on the edge of a main dirt road that wandered around through the valley. A story I heard growing up was the house was on land that had belonged to my great-grandfather and had actually been deeded to my grandfather. Somehow, Cicero had gotten into some sort of deal with Dad and wound up with a nice piece of land and the house. I don't know how true this story was because it was never discussed by anyone in the family, just those on the outside.

At any rate, Cicero was a businessman. He was married to Gladys, who was my mother's first cousin, as well as a first cousin to Aunt Maggie. Gladys was a piece of work, to say the least, as was Cicero. When I was about eight years old, Cicero moved his operation to an old Pure gas station right on Highway 11, about three miles from our house. He and Gladys lived in an apartment in the back of the business.

The store was as nasty as any you have imagined. It was crammed to the ceiling with all sorts of stuff. Food products were stuck between oil cans, old tires, guns, and various tools. This was an old-style country store that sold stick baloney and hoop cheese. An old Coca-Cola box dispensed cold drinks, and there were jars of crackers and nuts along the counter.

Racks of sundry items lined the wall behind the counter, along with a huge punchboard game. A punchboard is a low form of gambling that many small stores participated in from time to time. The board consisted of small holes with a thin paper covering them. Each hole was under a number, and certain ones contained a slip of paper with a prize listed on it. A punch cost maybe a dime or a quarter back then, and you could win money, tools, guns, and other lesser prizes. I have seen people come in and spend most of their paycheck on a punchboard. The board was rigged so that the storekeeper wound up the only big winner, so that was right up Cicero's alley. Cicero dealt in anything he could make a dime off of.

Rumor had it that if something was a little hot, it wouldn't matter to Cicero. And I know for a fact that he sold moonshine liquor because I helped him. He always had a supply of guns for sale, along with musical instruments and tools. You might say that Cicero operated sort of a pawnshop. Gladys was just as money conscious as Cicero, if not more so. Having said all that, both of them were good to me, even though they almost turned me into a young criminal. I spent many days after school cutting wood for Gladys. She would pay me fifty cents an hour, and I usually spent most of it back in the store. Some days I would help in the store, pumping gas or stocking shelves.

Then there were occasions when Cicero would have heard about a still or hiding hole for moonshine, and he would "hire" me to go raid the stash. There were many times that I snuck up to someone's hiding place and stole their 'shine. I took it to a new hiding hole, and after a day or two, took the jugs to Cicero. That's how I knew for sure that he sold 'shine. Interestingly, in all the time I knew Cicero and Gladys, they never tried to cheat me or beat me out of anything. Even stolen 'shine was paid for as promised. One time I raided some guys' homebrew still and took five gallons of brew ready for drinking. Homebrew is a god-awful-smelling and worse-tasting mixture of various fruits mixed with yeast and sugar. It ferments and turns to almost pure alcohol. Only a hard-core drinker or stone-cold alcoholic would drink the stuff, but I have heard from those who have, that it will turn you inside out and make you see things that are not there.

Cicero had an old bird dog named Cricket that was several pounds overweight and in bad health. This old dog slept in the bed with Cicero and ate out of the same plate. In his later years, Cicero suffered from severe diabetes and was almost completely crippled. He lay in bed almost all day with that old dog and would yell at Gladys about everything. The dog got treated way better than Gladys ever did, but she stayed right up to the end and never wavered from Cicero.

Among other things that Cicero paid me for was to bring him birds. He paid me ten cents for every dove or robin I killed. Back then, a box of twenty-two shells cost about thirty-five cents, and I could get a dime for every bird I shot. That made economical sense to me. I got to shoot all I wanted and, in turn, used what I killed to get more shells. It was a great arrangement. One time though, Cicero got greedy and wanted more than dove or robin. He had heard that someone down the road had some chickens running loose around the house, and he wanted them. He agreed to pay me fifty cents for every chicken I brought him, and I took him up on the deal. I snuck up on the house, saw that no one was at home, and the hunt was on. I shot maybe three or four of those chickens and hid them in a clump of cedar bushes until the next day. As soon as I got off the bus the next day, I recovered the stashed chickens and carried them through the woods to Cicero. I made quite a haul that day and had more money than I knew what to do with.

In a totally ironic turn of events, I was out one day roaming around with Mike, when we came upon some chickens running around wild in the woods pretty far from Cicero's. As always, we had our guns, and Mike thought it would be great fun to take a couple of shots at the chickens. For whatever reason, I chose not to participate, probably because I didn't want to waste ammo without being able to sell something as a result. Who knows? But at any rate, I didn't do any shooting. Mike shot maybe two or three of the chickens, and we went on our way. Now unbeknownst to us, the chickens belonged to Cicero. They were way out in the woods quite a ways from his store, and we never imagined that they might be his. We actually thought that they were wild.

A couple days after the shooting spree, my brother told me the county sheriff wanted to see me and that he was taking me to his office. I had never been to the sheriff's office before, but I knew who he was. He lived very close to me, and his daughter married one of my uncles. So I went into the office, and he proceeded to tell me that he knew all about the killing of the chickens and that they belonged to Cicero. He said that Cicero didn't want to press charges against me; he just wanted an apology. I told him that I hadn't shot the chickens and had nothing to apologize for. Well he got pretty mad and told my brother he had better talk some sense into me. This was serious business, and I was in a lot of trouble. I left his office, with my brother lecturing me all the way home and telling me how stupid I was. I told him the same thing I told the sheriff. I didn't shoot the chickens and wasn't about to apologize to anyone. I thought, *What a hypocrite! How many times had Cicero paid me to bring him chickens, 'shine, and other stuff that he knew belonged to someone else?*

When we got home, I told my mother what happened, and she said she would take care of it the next day. The next day after she got off from work at the laundry, she took a cab down to the sheriff's office, walked in, and demanded to see him. She told him that the next time he bothered her son, she would claw his eyes out and feed them to him. He must have believed her because I never heard another word about chickens. Several days later I confronted Cicero about it. He stammered around and told me some story about someone else turning me in. At any rate, our relationship soured for some time after that, and it took a while for me to get over the fact he called the law about something like that, especially when he didn't have the facts straight. I think Mike eventually went down to see the sheriff and actually paid for the chickens he shot.

Once a bus carrying some sort of big band from New York broke down right in front of Cicero's store. There must have been twenty-five or more men and women on the bus, and they were stranded there until the bus could be repaired. Old Cicero capitalized on their misfortune and turned it into a windfall for himself. He had Gladys bring a coffeepot down from their apartment and brew up some coffee—for which he charged, of course. She also brought a griddle and fried up some baloney sandwiches and scrambled eggs. In addition to the coffee and sandwiches, they bought us out of Cokes, chips, cookies, and nuts. I think that they ran the punchboard completely out, as they had never seen anything like that before and really got caught up in the gambling of it. Of course, Gladys immediately employed me to help take cash and fetch whatever they wanted. I must have stayed until eight or so and then had to walk home in the dark through the cemetery. I did make a handful of money that night, and working behind the counter was better than sawing wood out in the cold. I always wondered what those obviously upper-crust people from New York thought about all of us. They probably thought this was surely where rednecks come from! Nevertheless, they finally got the bus repaired and were on their way, leaving Cicero with a considerable amount of their money.

Another time that fortune fell in Cicero's lap was when a traveling band of gypsies conned him into letting them park their trailers all around the store. I am sure Cicero charged them ample rent for staying there, but this was not your ordinary crowd of folks. These were hard-core con men and con women who made their living traveling around the country, running cons and scams. Most of the men had numerous gold teeth, and all wore earrings long before it became hip to do so. These guys were right out of a movie or adventure book: dark skinned with long, greasy, jet-black hair. Many wore sort of a doo-rag, or bandanna, on their heads. On occasion, they spoke in some foreign language. One thing was for sure, they all drove very nice and expensive vehicles, pulling even nicer trailers for them to live in. They never stayed in one place too long, and this time was no exception, as they were gone in about two weeks.

It was fun and really interesting to sit around talking to these guys and hearing their stories. It was also interesting to watch Cicero and the cons plot against each other to see who the biggest con was. I really believe the gypsies were plotting to kill old Cicero and rob him because he couldn't keep his mouth shut about what he had and what he could do for them. He probably had them believing that he was worth a lot more than he really was. After a couple weeks, the gypsies decided to move on, and when I came by after school one day, they were gone. Cicero was still alive, so all was well that ended well. Cicero probably saved his own life because he always had a gun with him, and he let it be known that he did. Gladys was the same way and would constantly talk about how she had shot someone before or that she had shot at someone. I am sure these gypsy folk thought about all of that in assessing the situation. Whatever the reason, I was glad they were gone and that everyone lived through it.

When you read this, you might get the impression that I was a complete juvenile delinquent, involved in all sorts of criminal enterprises. The fact is that I was simply an unsupervised young man with no adult male guidance. Most of these tales of wrongdoing were short lived and opportunities to earn some pocket change. Cicero and Gladys always paid me some attention, and because of that, there was virtually nothing I would not do for them, as bad as that may sound. Looking back, I am probably lucky my illicit activities went no further than sneaking some bootleggers' 'shine or shooting some half-wild chickens.

Cicero lived a miserable life health wise. He suffered from severe diabetes, and his feet and legs were in terrible shape. He was bedridden or confined to a wheelchair for most of the time that I knew him. I never saw him walking around or out doing anything, and most of his time he spent yelling at Gladys. I never knew why she put up with him or why she was so subservient. I doubt it was out of love. Gladys would pull a gun on a man twice her size and have him licking her feet, but she would run like a puppy when Cicero yelled for her. She waited on him hand and foot, making sure that his meals were just the way he wanted them, and took care of any other details, no matter how unpleasant they might be. Cicero and Gladys did not have any children, or if they did, I never knew about it and never heard about any. I also don't know how long they were married, but based on what I heard, it was a long time.

Cicero died a few years after I stopped hanging around there. Gladys got everything, including the store and a very nice piece of land over in the valley. I don't know how much money, if any, she got, but I do know she sold the land pretty quickly after Cicero died and bought herself a new car. She started fixing up and taking care of herself, which was something that she had not done while taking care of Cicero. I lost touch with Gladys and never saw her again after I stopped coming around. I don't know what happened to her or where she moved to, but in spite of all the things that she had me do for her and Cicero, she was good to me. Even though she and Cicero conned a twelve-year-old boy into doing some pretty bad things and then turned him into the sheriff, they will always hold a special place in my heart.

CHAPTER 9

Janet Rose

When I was about ten or eleven years old, we received word that Uncle Jack was coming home and bringing a new bride with him. Jack had been married twice before and had been divorced for the past several years. He was stationed in Alaska with the army and being transferred to another post in the lower forty-eight. Anytime Uncle Jack came home was a big deal. Everything had to be perfect, and I had to be on my best behavior. Waiting on him to come was sort of like waiting on Santa Claus, and for whatever reason, I couldn't wait.

The day finally came for him to arrive, and we watched for his car all day. Finally, we spotted him coming around the bend and down the hill to the house. It was like the pope had arrived with everyone standing out in the yard, waving and carrying on until he pulled up and parked. Jack was driving his 1954 maroon Ford sedan and pulling a little, weird-looking foreign car that I learned later was a Volkswagen Bug.

When the car stopped, he got out and opened the passenger side door. Out came a tall, slender, blond woman. Janet Rose had arrived. Janet Rose was a woman of substance from Connecticut. In other words, she was a—gasp—Yankee. She stood there, surveying the sight before her and, I am sure, wondering just what she had gotten herself into. Janet Rose had grown up in a privileged household with all the perks that go with it. We were told that she had gone to boarding school as a young girl and to college at some all-girl finishing school.

She studied to be a teacher and was posted at one of the military bases in Alaska. She met Uncle Jack at the Officers Club and had fallen for his Southern charm and rakish good looks.

There is no telling what he had told her about us before they arrived, but whatever it was, it certainly wasn't what she saw. I don't know who was more shocked, me or Janet Rose. I am sure we looked like Ma and Pa Kettle of the movies to her, and I probably didn't help any. I was this wild-looking, shaggy-haired, skinny kid who routinely peed off the end of the porch and ran around half-naked most of the time. Janet Rose was this mysterious, fancy woman who talked funny. I am sure that she had never been inside a house with no running water or electricity and had certainly never gone outside to use the bathroom. Jack delighted in showing her around his property and especially enjoyed taking her down through the cemetery. He even talked either me or my brother into hiding down there with a sheet just to scare her when they went for a walk. This was getting more interesting by the minute—just watching her reaction to it all—and I can imagine some of the conversations they must have had.

She had to take baths in a wash pan, use an outhouse, and eat the most basic country cooking ever. I doubt Janet Rose had ever eaten a biscuit in her life, much less sawmill gravy or sorghum syrup. Janet Rose was determined to make the best of it, though, and really tried to get to know me. We had numerous conversations about school, grades, and what I wanted to do with my life. Unfortunately, I didn't know myself, and I am sure I came off as a real "bumpkin." She was always nice to me and took time out for me whenever they visited.

This is more than I can say for Uncle Jack. Except for the tricycle he bought me, he never paid me any attention at all. I was always in his way and obviously not worth his time. Years later, after I started to college, he came around and wanted to be my mentor. By then it was basically too late. I remember one time in particular that he hurt my feelings terribly. It was sometime after Janet Rose arrived, and I had found a tiny harmonica somewhere. In Alabama we called them French harps, but the proper name is the harmonica. This little harp was only one inch long and limited in the notes it could make. I learned to play a couple of real songs on this thing and thought I was really something because of it. I could play "On Top of Old Smoky" like a pro. I was sure that since Jack was an accomplished fiddle player with a beautiful tenor voice, he would surely be impressed that I had an interest in music. One day Jack was at the house, and I was going to show him my music ability. I started playing my little harp, and instead of praising me, he yelled at me to quit making so much racket. He said it annoyed him. I was devastated. My feelings were hurt beyond belief, and it took a long time to get over my mixture of shame, hurt, and total letdown. How easy it would have been to capture the heart and soul of an eleven-year-old boy and have him in the palm of your hand forever.

He kind of got his payback because in the years to come, Janet Rose became less impressed with his fiddle playing. She made him stop playing all together, and I never heard him play again. I don't know why he allowed her to take something away from him that he loved so much, but it sure wasted his talent.

Janet Rose stayed the course and hung in there. A few years after she showed up, Jack had the house remodeled and water and electricity put in. I always believed that she was the main reason. She could never believe people lived so primitively. But some of it might have been her reluctance to use the outhouse. Whatever the reason, it made life a little better for us, especially my mother.

Jack eventually retired from the army, and after a stint at selling insurance, went to the University of Alabama at Tuscaloosa. I am sure that Janet Rose was the inspiration for him to go, but he did it and wound up being a teacher himself. I have to admit that seeing him graduate from college, especially the University of Alabama, had a significant impact on me and was one of the main reasons that one day I would graduate from college, as well.

After many years of teaching and serving as a principal, Jack and Janet Rose retired to the same little farm that I grew up on. They built a nice house some distance from the one we lived in and lived there until Jack's death. When he died, Janet Rose moved away and deeded the home place to me. The Yankee had come full circle with me.

CHAPTER 10

Teebo

One of the most interesting and intriguing characters from my childhood years was a man that was known throughout the area as Teebo. Teebo's real name was Edgar, and he was the son of Anna and Nip. I never knew what Nip's real name was, but that was what everyone called him for as long as I knew him. I am sure he got the nickname from the fact that he liked to take a little nip now and then, as I witnessed numerous times when he visited Dad. Teebo got his nickname from some sort of bone deformity in one of his thumbs. The story was that he had a "T bone" and that evolved into Teebo over the years. What this malady really was I am not sure, but whatever it was forced him to wear a homemade leather sleeve over the afflicted thumb. It was sort of a glove finger held on by leather cords tied around his wrist.

Everything about Teebo was unusual, from his appearance to his mannerisms. He was a big man of maybe 6'5" or so, and he probably weighed 220 pounds, if not more. He didn't have an ounce of fat on his body, and he was strong as an ox. Teebo would be considered mentally challenged by today's standards and would probably be hospitalized in an institution. But back then, everyone just thought that he wasn't "right."

I don't think anyone knew for sure what was wrong with Teebo, but there were several speculations and stories about what might have caused his condition. One story was that Anna had been kicked by a mule while she was carrying Teebo, and this caused him to be "not right." Another speculation was that Teebo was the result of some incestuous relationship. Of course, no one had any proof of any of the stories, but they were the subjects of many conversations. Teebo had somewhat of an unusual appearance, and his complexion was yellowish and jaundiced. He was completely bald and had bulging eyes and thick lips. He didn't have a tooth in his head, as they rotted out years earlier. And he always wore a long-sleeved shirt, overalls, and an old dirty hat. He chewed plug tobacco and always had tobacco juice running down his chin and onto the front of his overalls.

Teebo could not read or write. If he had to sign anything, he simply made his mark. The mark, which was an X, constituted his signature, just the same as anyone's. He could talk, even though it was sometimes difficult to understand him, as he mumbled. He swore like a sailor and would say whatever was on his mind, no matter who was present.

The most interesting thing about Teebo was that in spite of the fact he couldn't read or write and had probably never spent one day in school, he could count money like a banker. Cicero, the most unlikely person on the face of the earth, had taught him this skill many years earlier. As far as I know, Cicero never cheated Teebo out of anything and threatened to shoot anyone he suspected of doing so. You could not fool Teebo when it came to money. He had it down pat. He could make change, tell you how much you owed him, tell you what something or some service cost, and a host of other simple tasks. I cannot imagine the patience that it took to teach him to count money, much less to the extent that he could not be cheated.

Teebo was a wanderer and spent most of his life outside. It is doubtful that he ever had a bath in his life, and he probably didn't care. Despite his somewhat scary appearance, I never knew of Teebo doing any harm to anyone, taking anything from anyone, or being involved in any wrongdoing. I don't know if he understood right from wrong, but he never did anything mean against anyone.

He worked hard at various odd jobs, mostly picking berries or making whips. When berries were in season, Teebo made considerable money picking for people like my grandmother and others. He picked all kinds of berries, depending on what was available. He picked blackberries, huckleberries, and blueberries. He knew where all the patches were and would go into places no one else would. I don't remember what he charged per gallon, but I seem to recall that it was about fifty cents. He would come by our house, and Nanny would tell him how many gallons she wanted. And sometime later, he delivered them.

When Teebo came to our house, he would just walk right in. He never knocked or announced himself. He just opened the door and went in. If you were getting dressed or undressed, it was too bad. He always went straight to the water bucket and took a drink right from the dipper. He put the dipper right back into the bucket when he was through, which drove Nanny crazy. No sooner was Teebo out the door than she was in the kitchen, pouring out the water and scrubbing the bucket.

About the only vice Teebo had, other than swearing, was telling tall tales. I don't know if this was a controlled or an uncontrolled act, but some of the things he talked about were pure fantasy. He talked for hours, if he had an audience, about driving someone's car on a wild adventure or pulling someone from a wreck just before the car burst into flames. Of course, all of these stories were laced with his brand of profanity, which spiced the tale even more. When the story was finished or he got ready to go, he left just as abruptly as he arrived. Just up and out the door with no good-bye or "See ya later."

Most of the time, Teebo walked everywhere, but on occasion, he would show up driving someone's team and wagon. He seemed to have a way with horses or mules, and they seemed to understand him more than most people. When he walked, it was with a purpose. He had a long stride, and it seemed as though his focus was straight-ahead. He could probably walk faster than most people could run.

During planting season, some of the local farmers hired Teebo to plow for them or do other farm-related work. But most of the time, he picked fruit for what living that he made.

Teebo also made extra money making various leather items, particularly buggy whips. He made other things out of leather, but whips were his specialty, and most of us boys owned one that he made. These whips were works of art. He cut the leather into long, narrow strips about the same length, wide at the top and narrow at the end. Then he plaited the strips into a whip. Plaiting is done by taking the strips and running them over and under one another while compressing the plait into a tight, compact, and smooth roll. Some people call this braiding.

When the plaiting was complete, he tied the whip to a long, slender, hickory rod, attached a piece of hay baling twine to the end, and frayed the loose end of the twine. This twine, or "popper," created the pop or "crack" when the whip was deployed. A good whip handler could make a sound louder than a rifle going off with one of Teebo's masterpieces. The hickory rod allowed a driver to deploy the whip over the backs of a team while standing in a wagon. I used mine to make the cracking sound and cut down daisies and other flowers with one stroke of my wrist. Teebo charged about a dollar for one of his custom-made whips. Back then it seemed like a lot of money for some of us, but it was worth every penny.

None of us boys were the least bit afraid of Teebo. We picked at him if we saw him out. He would cuss at us and then go on about his way.

He lived at home with Anna and Nip, until they got too old to take care of him. Then he moved in with his sister and her husband. I don't know when Teebo died or what the circumstances were, and I don't remember hearing about him ever being sick. I simply lost contact with this one-of-a-kind individual.

CHAPTER 11

Shorty

Down at the end of the road that went from Highway 11 around the cemetery and up to our house was an old log house. This house had at one time been part of quite an enterprise that included a truck stop café,, store, and overnight cabin rentals. The only thing left of the property during my younger years was the basement of the cafe and this log house. I don't remember ever seeing the cafe or store, but I heard stories about it growing up. One of the stories concerned the basement, which was full of nasty, scummy, standing water most of the time. The story was that when the cafe was in operation, the folks who ran it also sold whiskey and beer, which was illegal at the time. The basement had a dumbwaiter installed, going up to the main part of the business. When a customer wanted a drink, the server called down, and it was placed into the dumbwaiter and brought up. Supposedly there was a secret entrance to the basement, with a trap-door only a few people knew about. Whether this is factual, I have no idea, but everyone around there told the same story. So maybe it was true.

Over the years, numerous families lived in the log house. At one time it was a very nice home, but as renters came and went, the house became rundown and unlivable. After a couple of years of no one living in the house, Shorty came along and squatted. He just moved in and made himself at home without anyone's permission. I don't know where Shorty came from; he just showed up one day. I don't know if anyone really knew who he was, but it was obvious why he was called Shorty because he couldn't have been much over five feet tall. He was thin and wiry, with tanned skin and a rough complexion. Shorty was a hermit through and through, and today would be considered homeless. He never took a bath or shaved, and he wore the same pair of overalls until they came apart, at which time he would somehow get new ones. All his teeth were gone. He was mostly bald, except for around his ears and back of his neck, which sort of blended in with his beard.

Since there was no running water or electricity in the log house, Shorty walked up to our house every evening, just after sundown, to get water. He would bring two jugs tied to a pole he carried over his shoulder. He filled them up from the well and carried them back home. Most evenings Dad brought out the jug of 'shine, and he and Shorty sat on the front porch and told tall tales until way after dark. Shorty smoked, and he rolled his own cigarettes from Prince Albert or Country Gentleman, while Dad puffed away on his ever-present pipe. After a couple hours, Shorty said his good-byes and headed off through the woods to his home.

Shorty always carried an old, double-barreled shotgun with him everywhere he went. Some nights after he and Dad had been in the jug, he would fire off a couple rounds as he walked down the trail. Most evenings you could hear him singing and yodeling at the top of his lungs between the gunshots.

Somewhere I heard that Shorty was retired from something, but I never knew from what. It may have been the army or railroad, but I don't know for sure. He never talked about it where I could hear, but there were rumors that he received a check from somewhere, even though he never seemed to have money. Shorty may have served in World War I, as I remember hearing tidbits of conversation about fighting in a war. He told tall tales about being on the front lines and filling cannons with anything they could find, including pieces of trace chain, and firing it at the enemy. I never heard him say how old he was, but I would estimate that he was in his late sixties at the time, and I was maybe nine or so when I first saw him. I don't remember hearing about a wife or children, and if he had either, he kept it to himself. It was obvious that Shorty was quite an outdoorsman who knew how to survive off the land because he hunted and fished for most of his food, and I never saw him going anywhere to get groceries.

A friend and I broke into Shorty's house one day just to see what he lived in. He was living in one room of the old house, with only an old cot and a couple of small tables. There was no food stored or clothes hanging anywhere. The water jugs from our house were there, but little else.

I don't believe that Shorty and Dad knew each other before he started coming for water. They just seemed to enjoy sitting, sipping, and telling tales. This was very unusual because old Dad didn't take to strangers and sure didn't like sharing his 'shine with anyone. He and Shorty got along for whatever reason, and the relationship went on for a couple years or more, until one day old Shorty went crazy as a bedbug.

All those rumors about retirement had been true, and it appeared he had been saving his checks for years in a shoebox. I never knew what sparked Shorty to do the things that he did, but it was wild. He cleaned himself up, bought himself several new suits, and shaved off his beard. He went to a dentist and had false teeth made. The next thing he did, much to everyone's surprise, was to buy himself a car. I doubt that Shorty had ever driven a car before, but now he owned one. He bought a sharp-looking Pontiac and instantly became a man about town. It was like you were seeing a completely different person. He looked differently, talked differently, and certainly acted differently.

Shorty started to frequent some of the dance halls over in the next county, where it was legal to buy alcohol. Every now and then he was seen sporting around with a woman friend. I don't know how much money he saved up, but he was spending it like there was no tomorrow. And it was rumored that he would buy rounds for a whole bar full of people without blinking an eye.

But as they say, "all good things must come to an end," and it did for Shorty. One day he came tearing up to the house in his Pontiac and told us he had been out running around the night before, and the police had gotten after him. He had been drinking and, of course, didn't have a license, so the best thing to do was to run from the law. The police chased him all the way up Highway 11, close to our house, where he ducked down a side road and turned the lights off on the car. Apparently the police didn't see his maneuver and drove on by.

Shorty was certain they are going to turn around and come after him, so he jumped out of the car and started running across this big pasture, throwing away his shotgun, pistol, and a big wad of money as he ran. He left the car there and hiked through the woods until he felt safe and lay down for the rest of the night. Sometime later, when morning came, he slipped back down, found his car, and high-tailed it to our house. He enlisted me to go down and help him hunt for his guns and money, and I spent all that day walking back and forth across that pasture, looking for all his stuff. We found the shotgun and pistol but never did find the money. Of course, Shorty was so drunk at the time that he may have only thought that he threw it out. Who knows?

Once right after he started on his wild binge, he told me he was going to buy another car, and when he did, he would give me his old one. That would have been something, as I couldn't have been more than eleven then and would have had my own car. What a hoot! Of course, I would have been about as mature as that old drunk was and probably could have driven just as well. I do remember that he didn't give me anything for spending all day finding his guns and looking for his money, so I probably wouldn't have gotten the car, either.

Soon after his wild night, Shorty realized he had spent all of his money. So he sold the car and other stuff and disappeared. I have no idea where he went, but he moved from the old house without saying good-bye or anything. He just vanished. We went back inside the house one day, and the cot and tables were still there. But you could tell that no one was staying there. Even the water jugs were gone.

CHAPTER 12

New School, Elvis, and Holy Rollers

When I was about thirteen years old, Mother finally got up the courage to move to Fort Payne. This move was prompted by the fact that I got into a terrible fight with Dad over an old lawnmower. What started out as an argument wound up with us actually throwing blows. I realize now this was entirely the wrong thing to do and that he was my elder, who had provided me a place to live and food to eat. However, on that day, I had enough.

Soon after we had the fight, Mother rented a small house in town, and we moved in. I continued to attend the same school for the rest of that year, walking about three miles to catch the bus. At the beginning of the next school year, I transferred to Fort Payne School, and when I enrolled, I changed my name.

As I mentioned earlier, I wanted to get away from as much of my past as possible, especially my nickname. I immediately became somewhat of a punk, with a confident swagger and big talk. I smoked and would do anything to get attention, even if it was the wrong kind. I didn't seem to fit in anywhere. My grades were not good enough to belong to the Beta Club crowd, and I certainly wasn't a jock. So punk it was.

I wore my hair in the closest thing to a ducktail that I could and refused to tuck my shirttail inside my pants, even though it was the rule on campus. Whatever the rule was, I broke it. Some of my fellow punks and I brought firecrackers to school and set them off in strategic places. We especially liked cherry bombs, which are pretty powerful and can cause tremendous damage. We found out these little bombs would go off even wet, so we flushed them down the toilets. It just so happened that a flush from the boys restroom went past the girls restroom at just the right time for a cherry bomb to explode, sending water up out of the girls' toilets, causing general chaos. I am sure that our ill-thought-out prank caused untold damage to the plumbing. We never got caught, even though lots of people knew who was doing it.

Another favorite was to drop a firecracker into one of the trash cans that lined the hallway. These cans had flip-top lids and when the cracker went off, the lid would sometimes go flying into the air. Needless to say, a well-placed firecracker going off during change of class caused quite a panic. These were usually set off on our way out back to the smoking area to grab a quick cigarette.

The designated smoking area was in back of the school and right at the foot of the mountain. Years earlier, someone had planted kudzu up the mountain, hoping to reduce erosion by holding some of the dirt in place. Kudzu, for those folks who are not from the South, was imported from Asia years ago for the distinct purpose of controlling erosion. The problem is that kudzu grows like crazy, overtaking everything in its path. It will envelop and kill a full-grown oak tree in a just few short years. Kudzu is seasonal and dries up during the winter, only to come back to life once spring arrives.

So there we were, young punks standing out back—puffing away on our cigarettes, swapping lies about who had done the craziest things—when one of us came up with the bright idea of lighting off the kudzu. I don't remember who lit it. It may have been me, but I am not sure. I do know somebody did, and it went up like gasoline, with flames going fifty feet or so in the air. Fire trucks came rushing over, and school was closed for the day. What a success! Let's start planning for next year.

I discovered girls about this same time and had numerous girlfriends over the next couple of years, including the girl I ultimately married. I won't go into all the romances, nor will I kiss and tell. But I will mention a couple who in one way or another had a significant impact on my life.

One of those girls was Rodonna. She was much older than I. We met on a double date with a guy I had started running around with. She did not go to school and lived at home with her mother and daddy. The most significant thing about her was that she was an Elvis freak. She lived and breathed Elvis and started an international Elvis fan club. She ran the club right out of her house, and it was a no-kidding fan club with some renown. Her mother was as much of an Elvis nut as she was.

This was right about the time he was making all his movies and would spend about half or more of the year in Hollywood and the other half in Memphis. Rodonna and her mother knew from the fan club exactly when he would be coming home and made plans to travel to Memphis just to get a glimpse of him. They would take the Greyhound bus to Memphis, stay in a motel down the street from Graceland, and then walk to Graceland every day to wait until he came out or drove in from somewhere.

While Elvis was in Hollywood, they waited anxiously for his next movie to come out and then rushed to the theater to see it. Rodonna's daddy had an old car but hated to go to the drive-in and hated Elvis even more. No amount of persuasion would move him; he just wasn't going. So then I came along, and Rodonna and her mother concocted a way to get to the drive-in to see Elvis. Me! They talked the daddy into letting me drive them to the show. Daddy didn't have to go to the theater, Rodonna and her mother got to see Elvis, and I got to drive.

The only problem was that I was fourteen, didn't have a driver's license, and had never driven a car before. It was time to get out the *Funk and Wagnalls* and learn to drive. The very first time that I ever drove a car was to take Rodonna and her mother to see Elvis. The car was an old Ford with a stick shift on the column. After several tries, I managed to back it out of the driveway and head to the show. Somehow, I got to the drive-in and got us parked reasonably straight. Mother sat in the back, and Rodonna and I sat up front. It was sort of like double dating with your mother. Not much romance for sure, but Rodonna's mother paid for everything, which was fine with me. She and Rodonna spent the entire evening talking about the movie and how good Elvis looked or how well he sang. When the movie was over, I somehow got them back home, and after a short good night had to walk home. This went on for some time, and we went to every new movie that came to the drive-in.

Rodonna and her mother went to Memphis several times while I knew them, each time getting closer and closer to Elvis. They befriended someone in Elvis's entourage and slowly worked their way inside to meet him. By the time I ended the relationship, Rodonna and her mother were actually staying at Graceland with Elvis when they visited. He took them on outings along with his usual crowd and treated them like royalty. I would not have believed any of this except that Rodonna had hundreds of pictures taken with him at Graceland and other places. Over the years, he gave her numerous gifts and souvenirs that are probably worth a fortune today if she still has them.

One of the most important things I remember about our relationship was that Rodonna's mother was one of the best cooks I have ever known. She grew a garden and always cooked huge meals. Many times when we were going to the movies, I would get to their house early and eat supper there before we left. I guess it says something about a relationship when the main thing you remember about it was the food.

Many of the girls I dated seemed to have some affiliation with the Holiness or Pentecostal church. I certainly didn't look for them; it just seemed to happen that way. Several, including the girl I married, had fathers who were preachers. People of the Pentecostal faith are different from most churchgoers. Women don't wear makeup or jewelry. They wear very modest dresses and would never be seen wearing shorts or pants. The only jewelry either sex can wear is a wristwatch.

Most folks who were not of that faith called those who were "Holy Rollers" and gave them a wide path if they were encountered. People of the faith believe in the Holy Ghost, among other things, and to fully experience the faith you have to receive the Holy Ghost, which usually involves uncontrolled convulsing, shouting, and speaking in tongues.

I have witnessed things in the Holiness Church that most people would not believe. I have seen fire inside a church. Blue flame appeared around people's heads as they danced around the room and jumped up on the pews. The flame probably came from the intense energy generated by the cavorting. At one time, I traveled around with an evangelist, who happened to be the father of a girl I was dating. I played the guitar and sang, while he conducted tent meetings and prayer sessions. Another guy, who played the piano, also went along. We would get the crowd all fired up by playing and singing blues and rock until he came out to preach.

The funny thing was that most of these people were totally against rock and roll music. They believed it was the "devil's music," and anyone who listened to it was bound for hell. They sure got into it when we played, though. It seemed like the louder and faster we played, the more fanatic they became. It would start out with some hand clapping and singing along until the beat got stronger. Then they started screaming in tongues, which may have been important to them but sounded like babble to me. By the time we finished a song, they would be literally in a trance, convulsing uncontrollably, and totally oblivious to what was going on around them.

When the preacher started, he only had to say a few syllables over and over with a few "Halleluiahs" and "Praise Gods" thrown in, and the crowd would go even wilder. Every now and then, he paused and passed the hat. The more fired up people were, the more money they threw in. When we finished, we climbed in his old car, and he took me home until the next service.

Relationships come and go, however, and this one did, too. I moved on to other girls, but I carried a torch, so to speak, for this girl for a long time. Every day I thank God for unanswered prayers because that relationship would have been a disaster for sure.

I am not knocking anyone's religion, nor am I making light of the Holiness Church. I am simply relating some stories that happened during my life that were perhaps a little odd.

When I started dating the girl I eventually married, her father sat down with me one day and admonished me to never take his daughter to a drive-in or theater. It was pure sin, according to him, and not to be done. He told me there were plenty of other things young people could do together and suggested we go somewhere and park! "Let me get this straight, sir. You want me to go parking with your daughter out in some field somewhere, alone, under the stars? I believe that I got this, yes sir!" Fortunately, my wife-to-be had better sense than her daddy, and we really didn't take advantage of the parking offer. Several years later, after we were married, church elders told her that she had to remove the rings that I had given her because it was a sin and against the church laws for women to wear jewelry. She refused and was "turned out" of the church. We never set foot in that church again.

CHAPTER 13

My First Car

Shortly after we moved to Fort Payne, I started hanging around the Piggly Wiggly grocery store after school. A friend who lived next door to us had a job there, and I went by and cut up with him until he got off work. Through him I met the guys who worked in the meat market of the store, and after a while, they let me help clean up after the store closed. At first I only made some change that they threw in a hat, so to speak. But after a few weeks, they offered me a real job. I started working a couple nights a week and all day Saturday. I made $7.50 a week and thought I was surely in heaven. I cleaned the machinery, ground hamburger, wrapped meat, and did any other odd job the meat cutters needed done. After a few months of this menial labor, I started learning to cut meat myself. I started boning meat, cutting up chicken, and making the various cuts of steak and chops. Pretty good for a teenager!

I was living the dream and started thinking about buying a car. I had heard stories about the car auction just south of town that sold cars every Saturday night. I was told you could buy a car there for $50. It became my goal to save that amount and go get my own car. This would have been a normal occurrence, except for the fact I was only fourteen years old and wouldn't be fifteen for a couple of months. That did not deter me, however, and I managed to save up about $30. I went to the store manager and asked him to advance me $20 against my check, and to my surprise, he agreed. The very next Saturday I got off work about 7:00 p.m. and walked the six or so miles to the auction. I had no real idea of how to go about buying a car, so I just went in and watched for a few minutes to get the hang of it.

The auction was held in a huge building that had doors on both ends so cars could go in and get out. Rows of homemade bleachers lined both sides of the floor, and buyers sat there until a car they were interested in came through. If they were interested in a car, they could come down on the floor to get a closer look, raise the hood or trunk, and listen closely to the motor. The auctioneer was in charge of the selling process and hawked the cars with his rapid-fire chatter and rhythmic urging to bid. If the buyers wanted to bid, they simply raised a hand or made some other motion to the auctioneer or the floormen.

Most of the people in the room were car dealers, experienced in the car-buying business. Many had brought along a bottle or jug to help the evening along, and this was not the best place for a young teenager to be, especially alone. I was determined, however, to buy a car, and nothing was going to keep me from it. Most of the cars that went through were sold for several hundred dollars, and the few that started out in my price range soon sold for much more.

I was starting to get discouraged when an old, blue Oldsmobile came through. It was a 1954, four-door Olds with more rust on it than metal. The tires were worn and mismatched, but it ran like a clock and didn't smoke at all. I thought, *This is it.* Then the auctioneer yelled out the starting bid of $50. "Who will give $50, $50, $50? Gimme $50!" I raised my hand. "I have $50 over here," he yelled. "Fifty-five. Who will give $55? Going once, going twice, sold for $50." Then I heard, "Hold on. We have a no sale. The owner has rejected the bid!" I was destroyed. This was the last car of the night in my price range, and the owner wasn't going to sell it. I was going to have to walk home without a car.

After the auction, I started out the door and into the parking lot, ready to start on my way home, when I heard a man yell at me to come over. I went over, and he asked if I still wanted the car. Of course I did; dumb question. He looked around, kind of shifty-eyed, and said he had not sold the car because he didn't want to pay the auction fee. But he would sell it to me for the $50. I gave him the money, and he gave me the title to the car along with the keys. Thank God the car had some gas in it because by now, I was flat broke, spending everything I had for the car.

The old bomb didn't look like much, but it ran great and had a radio, even though it didn't work until I wrapped tin foil around the fuse. So there I was, fourteen years old, driving a car with no tags, no insurance, and no license. What could possibly be wrong with this picture? At least by now I knew how to drive, since I had been going to the drive-in for a few months and gotten the hang of it.

CHAPTER 14

Hugh John's and Jacks Hamburgers

I kept that old clunker for quite a while, driving it to and from school and work, until I got laid off from the Piggly Wiggly. I heard through another classmate that a little grocery store in town was looking for someone to deliver groceries and do stocking work full time, six days a week. School was out for the summer, so I applied and got the job. The grocery store was called Hugh John's Grocery, and the owner found a niche not found in the bigger-name brand stores. He delivered groceries to customers. You could call Hugh John and tell him what you wanted. He put the order together and his driver delivered it to you. Of course, Hugh John charged more for his merchandise, but enough customers thought it was worth it to keep him in business. Hugh John used an old Jeepster for deliveries. When he hired me, he never asked how old I was or whether I had a license to drive. I don't know if he just didn't care or didn't think of it, but he didn't ask, and I didn't tell him.

Many of Hugh John's customers were the older, more refined citizens of Fort Payne. Many considered themselves too busy or too good to spend time grocery shopping. I had keys to their houses or knew where they hid them, so I could go in anytime I wanted. After a while, I learned where the groceries went and exactly how they wanted them put up. I delivered the order, went inside, and put everything away as they requested.

Hugh John's was a full-service grocery store with a custom meat market. I was a real plus because of my experience at Piggly Wiggly. I could cut meat better than he could, and I filled many custom orders for him. I stocked shelves between orders or when there were no meat orders to fill. I enjoyed working for Hugh John, but when school started back from summer vacation, he wanted me to quit and continue working full time for him. I actually thought about doing that but in the end, decided to go back to school and quit the job instead.

Around that same time, a new drive-in restaurant was being built in town. They were hiring, so I applied. The restaurant, a hamburger stand, was called Jacks. I started there as a member of the "charter crew" and worked for several weeks, until Jack and I came to an understanding that it wasn't working out. I was working full time, six nights a week, and trying to go to school, and it was starting to get to me. I wasn't doing fantastically in school anyway, and it was getting worse while I worked there. So I parted ways with Jack on friendly terms.

The one thing I will say about that restaurant is that they served the best hamburger I have ever tasted anywhere. It was called the Bonanza Burger, and it was unique. He should have franchised the hamburger but never did. An unusual thing about the restaurant was that even though this was in the early sixties, Jacks was one of the last businesses in town to have a sign on the door reading, "White Only."

By the time that I left Jacks, I was sixteen but still didn't have a driver's license. I just never saw the need. I had been driving so long without one that I never bothered with taking the test.

I continued to struggle in school and somehow managed to have a little spending money now and then for dates. I met Gail sometime around midyear after I turned sixteen. She and I had classes together and somehow hit it off. She was slender as a rail but beautiful. She had the most piercing green eyes that I had ever seen in a girl. She and I started dating heavily and were inseparable. We were together constantly in class or out. Her daddy was a heavy-equipment operator working on the I 59 and was as mean as they come. He drank a lot and was a rough guy when he did. Her mother was a really sweet person who thought the world of me and made sure Daddy didn't kill me. They owned a beautiful Ford Crown Victoria and on several occasions actually let me take it on a date. It was with Gail that I double dated with Jean, who was my childhood sweetheart.

Gail was from Atlanta and was only here while her daddy was working on the highway. We always knew the day would come when she would go back home, and I might never see her again. Well that day came, and the date to leave was set. I was majorly depressed about facing life without her. I was still struggling in school, and this new development was not helping any. I started thinking about quitting school and joining the military as soon as I turned seventeen. I didn't see a future in staying around Fort Payne. Jobs were scarce, and any good ones required knowing someone in order to be hired. My life was a mess and getting worse by the day.

Gail was leaving, I didn't have a job, and I was failing in school. What more could happen? Well one day in class, Gail wrote a note and passed it to me, telling me something about her move. It probably was her address or phone number, but I don't know for sure because the teacher intercepted the note on its way to me. Instead of keeping the note until after class and then admonishing us, he took the note to the front of the class. He opened the note and started to read it out loud. I interrupted him, saying if he did, I would clean his clock. In other words, I threatened a teacher, which was a big no-no. It did stop him from reading the note and embarrassing both of us. However, he was not amused and took me straight to the principal's office. Mr. Smith, the principal, listened to the teacher but never let me say a word. When he heard enough, he turned to me and said, "There is no room for you in upper academia." Mr. Smith gave me a choice to quit or be expelled. Well I had enjoyed enough of higher education anyway, so I quit. It was midyear, school was about to let out for Christmas, and I would be seventeen in just a few days. It was time to move on.

CHAPTER 15

Dropout to Sailor

When I left Fort Payne High School, I never looked back. My direction was clear, and I knew exactly what I was going to do. I would turn seventeen in just a couple of weeks, and I started making plans to join the military. I had plenty of examples to follow, since all three of my uncles served in one military branch or the other, and my older brother served in the navy. I was leaning toward navy, but I had not decided for sure. Back then there wasn't a recruiter in every small town, like there is today. In Fort Payne, a circuit recruiter set up in the local post office every two weeks. As luck would have it, he had been there just days before my seventeenth birthday and would not be back for another two weeks. Two weeks is a life time for an anxious teenager, so I started making other plans.

I had learned there was a full-time recruiter in Chattanooga, which was about sixty or sixty-five miles north of Fort Payne. I wanted to get to Chattanooga as quickly as possible, so there was nothing to do but get out on Highway 11 and start hitchhiking. Hitchhiking has been around as a way to travel for centuries and back then was fairly commonplace. The idea is to indicate that you need a ride by extending your thumb toward the desired direction of travel. Drivers stop and offer you a ride, usually just for company. Today no one in their right mind would try it, but back then it was reasonably safe for both the driver and the hitchhiker. I had done considerable hitchhiking already in my life and had gone to Rome, Georgia, a couple of times, as well as other places close by. Soon after starting out, I had a ride all the way to Chattanooga. I don't remember who it was with or any specifics of the trip; I just know I got there. The driver let me out on the edge of the main part of town, and I asked around for directions to the recruiting office. Someone pointed me in the right direction.

The recruiting offices were located on a side street in downtown Chattanooga. They were lined up one after the other down the street. It just so happened that the navy recruiter was first on the block, so I went in. This was 1964, and the Vietnam War was just starting to build up. The draft was in place, and recruiters were having a hard time making their quota. When I walked in, there was a mad dash to get to me, and after some ruckus, I sat down with one of the recruiters to start the process.

The first thing that I had to do after filling out some preliminary forms was take the entrance exam, which was a general knowledge test to see if you had the intelligence to function in the navy. Not long after I finished the test, the recruiter came back and told me that I did well on the test, but he had noticed I was only seventeen years old. I told him that he was correct, and that I was, in fact, just seventeen. He told me my parents or guardian would have to sign papers for me to enlist. I replied, "Not a problem. My mother will sign for me." He hesitated a moment and asked me if I was sure. I answered, "Yes, I am sure." He said, "See that station wagon out there? Get in it."

He asked me where I lived, and I told him Fort Payne, Alabama. He took me all the way back to Fort Payne, and we went into the laundry, where my mother worked. He had an armful of papers and kept mumbling that he sure hoped I was right about her signing. Mother came out, and he explained why he was there. Just as I had told him, she signed for me to enlist in the US Navy. I really believe that she was relieved because deep down, she knew I was headed for trouble if something didn't happen soon.

The recruiter reached into his pocket and handed me a ten dollar bill. He said that he wanted me to take the Greyhound bus to Chattanooga the following Thursday and didn't want me out hitchhiking. I was to meet up with some other fellows who were joining, and we would all go by bus to Nashville for processing.

When Thursday rolled around, I put his ten dollars into my pocket, packed a small travel bag with a few things along with a carton of cigarettes, and stuck out my thumb. His ten dollars was all the money I had in the world, and I wasn't about to spend it on a bus ticket. I made it to Chattanooga just fine and met up with several other guys who were joining. After some brief introductions, we were put on a charter bus headed to Nashville.

When we got to Nashville, we were taken to a big hotel close to the processing station and put up for the night. The next morning we started the arduous process of enlisting. There were more tests to take, physicals, mental evaluations, and at last, the oath of enlistment. All of this took three or four days, and when we were through, the ones who made it were taken to the Nashville airport for the flight to San Diego, California, and basic training.

When we got to the airport, I boarded the first airplane that I had ever seen up close. I had no idea what it was like to fly in a plane, so this was a big adventure for me. The plane was a big, old, four-engine, turbo-prop airliner that sputtered and roared to life once everyone got on board. After a long, tiring flight, we finally made it to San Diego. A bus picked us up at the airport and took us out to the naval training center, where we were going to live for the next nine weeks. I had no idea what lay in store, but I would soon find out.

Once we got inside the center, the bus stopped at the edge of a huge parking lot. A mean-looking, snarling guy came on board and ordered us to get off the bus and line up outside. Once we were off, he grabbed a big bucket of cigarette butts and started slinging them all over the parking lot like a mad man. When he finished, he yelled at us to get busy picking them up. When we finished picking up every last one and had put them back into the bucket, he grabbed it and slung them around again. After about the fourth or fifth time doing this exercise, I began to wonder just what I had gotten myself into. We were finally released from this nut case and formed into companies to start training.

Navy basic is considerably easier than that of the army or marine corps, but at the time, we thought we were surely going to die. I realized how good we had it when one day we were marching around on the parade field, and I noticed some marines training at the facility next to us. There were maybe eight or ten guys carrying a telephone pole over their heads and running at full speed around the field. After that, I figured I could hang with what we were doing.

Early in basic training, or boot camp, everyone receives shots for every conceivable illness known to man. At the time, the shots were given with an air gun. The serum was mixed into a large drum, and the entire apparatus was connected to a pump that forced air out of a tiny nozzle and into our arms. We would line up single file and march through a gauntlet of young medics, who were giving the shots. There would be one on one side and one on the other. When we got to the medic, he wiped our arms with some alcohol and pressed the gun to our arms. The gun made a high-pitched whining noise, and the serum was forced into our skin. If someone flinched or otherwise moved, he could be seriously injured, as the air would cut right through almost anything. It was not uncommon to see guys bleeding profusely after making it through the line. The hardest part of the process was listening to the sound of the guns as the shot was administered.

Another part of the early processing was a complete dental exam. We had all undergone physicals during the initial processing at Nashville but not a dental checkup. When I sat down in the chair at the dental clinic at seventeen, it was the first time I had ever been to a dentist. Dental hygiene was not high on my family's list of priorities. My mother was too stubborn and too poor to worry about things like that. All of her teeth had rotted out, as had both grandparents', so why worry about mine? There were many years we did not use any kind of toothpaste. We cleaned our teeth as best we could with a sweet gum stick. Later, brushing consisted of baking soda and salt (not necessarily the best treatment for cavity prevention).

When the dentist looked into my mouth, he just stamped "disaster" on my chart and moved on to the next sailor. Soon after basic training, I started on a quest to get all my teeth fixed. Over the next few years, the military spent hundreds of dollars saving most of them.

Our company was a mixture of guys from all over, from Alabama to California and everywhere in between. There was only one black guy in the whole company. His name was Carter, and he fit right in from the beginning. No one treated him any differently than anyone else. He was the first black person I had ever been around, since Alabama was still pretty much segregated at the time. Carter hung in there, and we all made it to graduation day.

Basic training brought a lot of firsts for me. I already mentioned I had my first flight getting to California. I saw the ocean for the first time as I landed in San Diego, and I ate things in the chowhall that I had never even heard of.

I had been to a theater before to see a movie, which was more than one guy in our company had done. He was from deep in the woods of Tennessee and as backward as they came. The company commander called him Country from the beginning, and Country had never been to a movie in his life. Later in our cycle, he slipped off one weekend, made it down to the base theater, and saw his first movie. He was like a kid who had tasted candy for the first time. For me, my status just went up several points, as there was someone in the Company who was more of a hick than I was.

From the very first day of basic I was behind the eight ball because I had not completed high school. There were guys in the company who had gone to college, and most had completed high school. The more-educated guys were picked for leadership positions right away, leaving the rest of us at their mercy. I tried as hard as I could to get attention, but I always seemed to catch the wrong kind. I wanted to be one of those guys who got to wear "Recruit Petty Officer" stripes on his uniform, and one day I got my chance. Men were picked from the various companies to be brigade staff officers for parades and formations. These staff positions carried recruit rank with them and were highly sought after.

One day someone came to our company looking for guys to fill these positions. As it turned out, one of the requirements was to be tall. Well that fit me to a tee, since I was 6'3", and I got to try out. Several of us were selected and taken to the parade field. The tryout consisted of, among other things, how well we looked in uniform and how well we could march. A series of drills were used to find just the right person for the assignment. After going through several of the guys, it was my turn. I was given the command, "left face," and I immediately turned right. I had suffered a severe brain cramp and was so excited just to be there that I had completely blown it. Needless to say, I wasn't selected and was immediately ordered back to my company.

Somehow, I picked up the pieces of what was left of my ego and managed to complete basic training. Basic really wasn't all that hard once I got past being homesick. The most physical part was the endless marching up and down the concrete "grinders," which were just big parking lots without any cars.

Every sailor stood watch several times during the cycle. While on watch, we had to really look out for senior noncoms or officers slipping up on us. There were all sorts of things that had to be memorized and kept at the ready for one of these guys who might come up on you and try to catch you off guard. Such things as "general orders" had to be given verbatim and without thinking. Failure to do so could result in push-ups or worse, such as being placed on report to your CO. Of course, such orders had to be given while standing at rigid attention, eyes straight-ahead, and in a certain way. Everything began and ended with, "Sir." If the NCO or officer detected the least bit of intimidation, he capitalized on it at your expense. If you answered correctly and with confidence, most of the time they would go away and leave you alone. My company won many awards during the nine weeks and graduated as the "Brigade Company."

The only thing I cared about at graduation was getting home. My flight to Atlanta wasn't scheduled to leave until the day after graduation, so I, along with several other members of our basic company, decided to go to Tijuana, Mexico. Tijuana is a rough border town just south of San Diego, and at the time, was off limits to US military personnel. That meant we weren't supposed to go there and also that it was off limits for a reason. The reason it was off limits was that Tijuana was a dirty, anything goes town, with a reputation for kidnapping and robbing sailors. It was also known for cheap booze, wild times, and ladies of the night. So nothing would do except go see for ourselves.

The first problem to overcome was that we didn't own any civilian clothes. And since Tijuana was off limits, it would be difficult to go there in our brand-new white uniforms. The solution to this problem was that just outside the gates of the naval training center, you could rent civilian clothes for an evening. We rented clothes and secured our uniforms in a locker at the facility. Then we boarded a bus for the short ride to the US–Mexican border.

We made it across and hailed a taxi to take us into town. Going to Tijuana at all is crazy enough considering the reputation and the fact that it's off limits, but I went with a small fortune in my pocket. We were not paid the entire time we were in basic mainly because there is nowhere to spend money, and it would not be practical to keep it in the barracks. So I was given three months of basic pay, travel pay, and per diem in cash when I cleared the training center. This came to over eight hundred dollars, and in 1964, that was a lot of money. I should have left at least part of the money in the locker with my uniform, but I chose to take it all with me. I am sure that at the time, one could have someone killed for a couple of dollars, so this kind of money was an attractive target.

We went to Tijuana and had a great time. We ate, drank, danced, and partied like rock stars. The main thing is we all made it out of there with most of the money we came with and lived to tell about it. Trust me when I say this Alabama country boy saw things that he had never seen before and has not seen since.

After basic I was sent to Philadelphia, Pennsylvania, for aviation—A—school. Even without a high school diploma, I scored high enough on the entrance tests to get a school and was sent to aviation boatswains mate fuels school to learn to fuel airplanes. I was hurt pretty badly during a school training exercise, when a jet turned into me. I was standing beside the runway, and the plane blew me, head over teakettle, down the tarmac. The accident tore all the ligaments in my right knee, and I could barely walk for several days. I didn't go to the doctor at the time but continued to have problems. The knee would just pop out of place for no reason and swell up like a basketball. I tried to just gut it out, hoping it would heal itself. At least once a month I would get careless, and the knee would snap. I didn't realize until much later that I was doing permanent damage to the knee by putting off seeing a doctor and having it repaired properly.

Going to school in Philadelphia was one of the more interesting experiences of my navy tour. That was the first time that I had spent any real time in a big city, and it took some getting used to. Philly is an interesting place because of all the history but for us, it was just a big melting pot of all sorts of interesting people. The city courthouse sits right in the middle of town, and two streets run through it. Vehicle traffic goes around the courthouse, but pedestrian traffic walks through the building. Inside the building was a huge open area that served as a hangout and a place to pick up girls. On any given night, you could hear some of the best singing in the world. Most nights there was at least one doo-wop group practicing their chops. And if they were good, there would be a huge crowd gathered around. I often wonder if any of the groups I heard actually made it in the business.

While I was going through A school, I met and befriended a guy from Silver City, New Mexico, and one day we decided to take a train to New York. This was another first for me, as I had never ridden on a train before and certainly had never been to the "Big Apple." We made it there just fine. While we were there, we visited the Empire State Building and afterward went to the 1964 World's Fair.

My friend had a sister who lived just outside of Philly, and after a couple of phone calls to her, she invited him to visit. He invited me, so we hopped another train and took off. The guy's brother-in-law was a college professor at a prestigious all-girls college. He came to the train station and picked us up. After a short drive, we arrived at their home. These folks rolled out the red carpet for us and went out of their way to make me feel welcome. We spent the entire weekend with them and had a blast. Sunday afternoon, the brother-in-law took us back to the train station for the trip back to base. I am sad to say I have no idea who these people were, and I have long forgotten the name of my friend. I regret not staying in contact with him and his family.

About midway through the A course we moved to Bayonne, New

Jersey, for training. Bayonne is a dirty, port town right across the bay from New York. It is industrial, and the folks who live and work there tend to be no-nonsense kind of people. Prior to leaving for Bayonne, I obtained a fake driver's license from somewhere that said I was twenty-one, which was the legal age to drink at the time. I couldn't wait to try out my new-found freedom, so as soon as we had weekend liberty, I headed for downtown Bayonne. I found a little bar on the waterfront and went in. The bartender was a big, old, burley dude who could have passed as a professional wrestler. He looked me over and asked for my ID to see how old I was. He checked me out pretty well, and in the process asked me what I did for a living. I told him I was an over-the-road truck driver, just in town long enough to drop a load and head out. He seemed satisfied and asked me what I wanted to drink. I obviously hadn't thought this out very well and really didn't know what to order. The only drink I could think of was a daiquiri! I noticed that he looked at me sort of funny after that, but he brought the drink anyway. It wasn't until sometime later that I found out a daiquiri is typically a lady's drink, and no self-respecting man would ever order one, especially a truck driver in a New Jersey bar.

CHAPTER 16

Life on the *Sara*

After A school, I was assigned to the USS *Saratoga,* an aircraft carrier berthed at Mayport, Florida. The Saratoga (CVA-60) was a huge vessel, 1,063 feet long, and carried a crew of over five thousand men. The *Saratoga* was built in the mid-1950s and commissioned in 1956. She was literally a floating city, with all the amenities a person would need to survive. Living conditions aboard the *Sara* were spartan, to say the least. Sleeping areas were cubicles with nine bunks per cube. The bunks were stacked on top of each other with three on the right, three on the left, and three in the front. The bunk area consisted of the bunk, or rack, and a small wall locker with just enough room for a set of uniforms. This tiny space was home away from home and held everything one owned. It quickly turned into a gaggle if general quarters was ever sounded, and all nine men had to get up and dressed at the same time. We really had to put aside any inhibitions we had as soon as we came aboard. Everything was done in the open, including showering, and there was never any privacy.

When the *Saratoga* sailed with all her aviation assets on board, she was a formidable military threat. I worked primarily on the flight deck, fueling planes. This was, without question, the most dangerous job that I have done in my life. The flight deck is a swirl of activity, taking place within three lengths of a football field, with planes landing and taking off at the same time. Landings are accomplished by the aircraft catching a wire that is stretched across the rear of the deck. It's somewhat of a controlled crash. There are propeller-driven aircraft mixed with jets and a few helicopters thrown in just to make it interesting. This is dangerous enough in the daytime, but at night, it is especially dangerous. Night flight operations require total blackout conditions, and the only light available comes from a red lens flashlight. We wore hoodies, goggles, and Mickey Mouse ears for hearing protection. The field of vision is minimal, you can't hear, and there are aircraft everywhere. Jet intakes are sucking, prop and jet wash is pushing, and props are turning. I dreaded night ops more than anything I ever did on the ship. I spent twenty-six months on the *Sara,* making two "Med" cruises to the Mediterranean Sea as well as numerous shorter voyages to San Juan and Cuba.

Here I was, seventeen years old, on my own, and seeing the world. By the time I was eighteen, I had seen more of the world than most people will in a lifetime. I had been to every country that borders the Med and seen and done things that are fantasies for most people.

One adventure stands out, though, and warrants further discussion. We were in Cannes, France, and for months had heard stories about a nudist colony that was supposed to be on one of the two islands some distance at sea. You could see both of the islands on a clear day, but they were a long way off. This did not deter five teenagers determined to find the colony. So we went ashore and rented two small paddleboats and a kayak. Two guys shared each boat, and one lone guy paddled the kayak. Out to sea we went in search of the nude women who were just over there, waiting for us. We didn't have food or water when we started off, but we did take a couple cases of beer. We paddled for hours, until we finally reached the shore of the island. We beached our little boats and started through the woods, not having a clue where anything was or even if there was anything. We just started walking. After a few minutes of walking in the deep woods, we came upon a young girl lying on a blanket, stark naked. Halleluiah! We found the "promised land!" When she saw us, she jumped up, grabbed her clothes, and ran off into the woods.

We thought if there was one, there were bound to be others. So we started off in the direction she ran. After a short while, we began to hear voices and soon discovered we were coming to a small town. There was a pub on the corner there, so we thought that would be an ideal place to get our bearings and find out about the nudist colony. After a few drinks, we finally found someone who spoke English and inquired about the location of the colony. It turned out that there was no nudist colony, and no one there had a clue of what we were talking about. There was nothing to do now but head back to shore, turn in the boats, and go back to the ship. When we headed back, it became apparent just how far we had paddled because we could just barely see the beach of Cannes in the distance. We finally made it back to ship, dead tired and thoroughly disappointed that we didn't find the colony. We never did figure out exactly what the girl was doing in the woods. Maybe she was waiting for her beau to show up and had gotten a head start. Who knows?

My time aboard the *Saratoga* was full of ups and downs, adventures, and misadventures. Looking back, I guess I did pretty well, considering that I was a seventeen-year-old kid from Alabama and thousands of miles away from home. I got into some trouble now and then but nothing serious. I worked hard for the most part and really tried to do a good job. Most of the time, trouble found me. Like the time that the division chief ordered me to make coffee for the officers. I dutifully took the pot and filled it with water, put in the coffee, and turned it on. After a few minutes, the little light came on indicating the coffee was ready. All the old "salts" came running with their cups, ready for their morning fixes. One of the officers took a sip from his cup and spit coffee across the room. Yelling and cussing followed. Out came the chief, looking for me. I was summoned to the office and stood at attention while the division officer ran up one side of my rear and down the other, chewing and spitting. After the smoke cleared, I found out that I had made the coffee with seawater instead of potable water. Now how the hell is a boy from Alabama supposed to know that? It never occurred to me that one of the faucets would be salty seawater! Well needless to say, they never told me to make coffee again.

Another time several of us were on liberty somewhere and were downtown in a bar. One of the guys we were with had a reputation of being a tough guy who liked to fight, and it didn't take much to get him started. There was another sailor, sitting with a very pretty woman at a table in the back of the room. He was minding his own business and just enjoying the evening, when the guy who liked to fight told us that he was going to mop the floor with him and take his girl. Now the smart thing for us to do would have been to get out of there fast. But we weren't that smart, so we stayed. The fighter guy told me and another guy to watch the door to make sure that the shore patrol wasn't around while he took care of the poor guy with the girl. We went over and stood just inside the door, while he went over to the guy's table with a full beer in his hand. He never said a word, just threw the beer in his face and started punching. All hell broke loose, and they were down on the floor, swinging and biting like mad, when someone yelled that the barkeep had called the shore patrol.

I might not have been smart, but I wasn't crazy either. So the other guy watching the door and I ran like hell. Life was going good, and it looked like we had made a clean getaway when we suddenly realized that we had run right back around the block to the same bar. Shore patrol was everywhere, and since we were running, they thought we must be involved in some way. So we were arrested. They took us down to the shore patrol headquarters and grilled us about our involvement in the assault. These guys were really getting up in our faces, and my friend was starting to get nervous. Now shore patrol officers are not police officers; they are regular sailors assigned the extra duty for a specific period. Most of them would rather be on the other side if they had a choice.

Our dilemma now was how to get out of this jam, and the answer came to me. When the guy started asking me what we were doing in the bar, I remembered something I saw on television. I answered as boldly and confidently as I could, "I stand on the Fifth Amendment." He asked me another question, and I answered the same thing" "I stand on the Fifth Amendment!" The shore patrolman looked at me and asked, "What the hell does that mean?" I said, "I don't have to answer any questions that might incriminate me." He sure didn't know what I was talking about and didn't know if what I said was true. He just stood there, flabbergasted, and couldn't say anything. The guy with me followed my lead and figured if it worked for me, it should work for him. When he was asked a question he said the same thing. So the shore patrol officer just shook his head and told us to get the hell out of his sight. We had enough adventure for one night and readily agreed to go straight back to the ship and promised never to come back into that town again. On the way back to the ship, he asked me how I knew that would work. I told him I didn't, but it was better than nothing. And it was all I could think of at the time.

I survived the majority of the first of two Med cruises but about two months from going home, my knee popped out to the point of requiring surgery. I was flown to the naval hospital in Naples. The surgery itself was fairly quick and was over within a week after arriving at the hospital. What took so long was the recovery time. Finally, the knee was well enough to catch up to the *Sara* for the trip home. I don't remember how or where I caught up with her, but I know she was steaming for home.

One of the most memorable events in making a Med cruise is going through the Straits of Gibraltar and meeting your replacement ship as she heads into where you are leaving. At the time, the navy made a big deal out of the event and threw a party for the sailors who were headed home. We were within a short distance from the Rock of Gibraltar, which is a huge mountain of sheer granite. There have always been rumors of what is hidden inside the rock, but on that day, it really didn't matter because home was just a couple weeks away.

The trip home was long and boring. About halfway across the Atlantic, all the aviation squadrons flew off and headed home. With all the aircraft gone, we were left with basically nothing to do but sit and watch the ocean go by and dream of what we were going to do once leave started.

At last the trip was coming to a close, and the only thing left was to "man the rail." This is a custom as old as the navy itself. When a ship leaves or returns to home port, the crew lines up on the edge of the flight deck in either the dress white or dress blue uniform and stands at a sharp "parade rest" until the ship is securely docked. Smaller ships man the rail around the bow and stern of the ship in basically the same manner. From a distance, it is quite impressive to watch. From up close, as a participant, it is a gaggle of anxious sailors just itching to get off the ship.

My leave started shortly after we were tied up at the dock, and I headed for Alabama. It was around the first of December 1965, and I would be married in just a few days. I have already written about that fiasco, so I won't belabor it here except to say I have no idea why I wanted to get married so badly. I was just days away from my nineteenth birthday, with my whole life ahead of me. I was seeing the world, but the only thing on my mind was getting married, preferably as quickly as possible. We didn't have a cent to our name when we married, and she had one more year of high school left. When my leave was up, we said our tearful good-byes and I headed back to the ship.

I managed to get home a couple of times in the next few months, but it seemed like no time had passed when I had to leave for the Med again. In just a short time, we were back on station, doing the same routine as before. I missed my wife's senior prom and her graduation, as both took place while I was away on the *Sara*. Schools in Alabama at that time were almost as backward as the church my wife belonged to when we married. Her high school wasn't used to having a student get married while still in school, and they really didn't know how to handle it. They made her jump through all sorts of hoops just to stay in long enough to graduate. She basically had to get special permission just to finish school, and they would have rather she quit school than to go to school married. It is no wonder that Alabama was on the bottom educationally at the time.

She managed to finish and graduate in spite of the administration and soon found a job working as a waitress for a local café. It wasn't much of a job, but for Fort Payne, it wasn't bad, either. I sent money home in the form of an allotment check, and she managed to get by.

About two-thirds of the way through this cruise, I got hurt again. Same story, different day! I spent quite a while in the ship's sick bay, until one day they decided to send me back to Naples. This time I flew directly off the flight deck of the *Sara,* which was an exciting experience. We were not shot off the deck by catapult, as most of the planes were. We just lumbered off the end of the deck and fortunately had enough lift to fly. Within a few hours, I found myself right back in the same hospital as before. After a couple of weeks, the doctors there decided that I should go back to the States and go before the medical board for evaluation. This was fine by me, as anything in the States was better than where I was.

While I was waiting for a flight out of Italy, I received word from the Red Cross that my grandfather had passed away. You might think I would be glad to hear that, considering our relationship over the years. But he was the only father figure I had ever known, so it stung a little. At first the command in Italy wasn't going to let me come home for the funeral, since he was only a grandparent. But the Red Cross intervened and set the commander straight. Within a couple of days I was on my way. The first flight got me to Rota, Spain, and another delay. I have no idea what happened, but I wound up assigned to a tugboat while waiting for a flight to the States.

I piddled around for a few days, painting and scrubbing floors, until I was finally notified that I had a flight. The flight turned out to be on a C-130 mail plane that was going to take forever to get to the States. The plane was a big, old, slow, lumbering prop plane that had been a military workhorse for decades. It could land and take off almost anywhere and was ultra-reliable. The only problem with the airplane was that it was slow! I stayed with the plane until it made a pit stop at Rhine Mien Air Force Base, Germany, and then went into the terminal and asked about any other flights going to the States. As luck would have it, there was a 707 leaving early the next morning that would arrive in New Jersey a couple of hours before the plane I was on. I opted for the 707 and settled in for the night, sleeping on a bench in the terminal. I awoke the next morning, grabbed my bags, and boarded the flight to New Jersey.

It turned out that the flight was a MATS (military air transport system) flight, carrying civilian dependents back to the States. I settled in and reflected on how much more comfortable the commercial plane was than the old cargo plane I had been on. The C-130 had huge piles of mailbags on board and was extremely noisy. There were no cute flight attendants on board, either.

The flight to Jersey lasted maybe eight or so hours. Before long, the pilot came on and notified us that we were twenty miles out and on final approach. No sooner had the pilot finished speaking, the plane filled with dark, thick smoke. There was panic everywhere, with people screaming and praying. The pilot came on again and said we were approaching the runway in emergency mode and to assume crash position. We were instructed to leave the airplane through the emergency doors as soon as we landed, go down the chute, and get as far away from the plane as possible.

A small child was playing in the aisle just as this happened, and there was no time to find his parents. I got him into the seat beside me and buckled him in. We were instructed on how to assume the crash position, which was basically putting your head between your knees. I thought, *If I am going to die, I at least want to see what was going on.* So I looked up and out the window as we were coming down. There were fire trucks everywhere, and ambulances and crash trucks lined the runway.

We touched down and immediately came to a stop. Someone pulled open the doors and activated the emergency chutes. I grabbed the little boy and hit the chute with him in my arms. Now I had to find the mother and get away from the plane at the same time. Fortunately, it didn't take long until she scooped him up, and we ran from the plane. She never thanked me or spoke to me at all. I really didn't expect her to, but it would have been nice. I never saw her or the child again. I found my way to the terminal and after some wait, retrieved my bags. We found out later that there was an electrical fire in the baggage compartment. There was a lot of smoke but no fire. Regardless, it was an experience I will never forget.

I called my wife and found out the funeral had already taken place. I was outraged! Everyone knew that I was on my way, and they were getting constant updates from the Red Cross. One of my uncles, who had made himself the family spokesperson, made the decision to go ahead and not wait on me. I never forgave him for that.

After getting this bit of news, I called my mother. I had not spoken to her in almost a year because of her reaction to my marriage. When she came on the phone I told her that I was bringing my wife there and expected everyone to be cordial to her. I told her in no uncertain terms that if she wasn't treated well, no one there would ever see me again. Mother agreed and actually kept her word.

After my leave was over, I reported to the naval hospital in Memphis, Tennessee, and started the process to determine my fitness for continued active duty. The medical board decided that I should return to active duty. At one point, it looked like I might be permanently transferred to Memphis. When I left the hospital, I was assigned to the crash crew at the airfield and tasked with driving a huge water truck. Working with the crash crew had its perks, for sure. I could go to the head of the chow line at any time, and we worked twenty-four on and twenty-four off. When we were working, we stayed at the firehouse for the entire twenty-four hours, unless we got called out on an emergency and then went home for twenty-four hours.

I was so sure I was going to be assigned to Naval Air Station Memphis that I applied for base housing and got it. Go figure! It usually takes years to get into base housing at my rank, but I did it in a couple of weeks. I was actually assigned a house in the enlisted neighborhood. One night I decided to drive by and take a look at our new home. I had the keys, so I stopped and looked the house over. While I was there, a couple of guys came by, introduced themselves, and said they lived in the neighborhood and wanted to welcome me. We stood around making chitchat when one of them said they belonged to a neighborhood club and wondered if I would be interested in joining. I had no idea what they were talking about, so I inquired about the club. One of them told me that it was a "key" club. Members met at one of the other member's house on weekends for a party. During the party, members' wives put their house keys into a hat, and male members drew a key from the hat. Male members went home with the woman whose key they picked. "So this is a wife swapping club," I said. "Yes it is," they replied. I thought, *My new wife ain't never gonna go for this.* She was a preacher's daughter, who was brought up in the Holiness

Church with all sorts of hang-ups. It also didn't sound right to me, even though I was only nineteen. I didn't have a lot of experience in such matters, but I had sense enough to say no. "Naah," I replied," I will pass on the invitation. Thanks for the invite though."

CHAPTER 17

Rufus and Lt. Junior Grade Lawrence

There are two people in my life to whom I give a lot of credit for being where I am today. They are men who had an extraordinary impact on my life. Either man could have just let life go by without giving me one second of thought, but they didn't, and I will be forever in their debt. I will try my best to tell their story here, but the truth is there is nothing I can say that will do justice for what they mean to me. Sadly, neither person has any idea of their impact on my life or my being here today.

Just as I was preparing for the move to Memphis, I came down on orders for Jacksonville, Florida. I was being assigned to a submarine patrol squadron that flew P3 Orion aircraft and was most likely going to deploy to Vietnam soon. I gathered all my stuff and went home on leave in preparation for the move. My wife and I packed what few belongings we had into our little Corvair and headed to Florida. We moved into a tiny apartment a couple of miles from base and started our happy home.

About this time, I got the wild idea that I wanted to start a business. Some people we knew back in Fort Payne operated a used clothing store, and I thought that was a great idea for Florida. The problem was I knew nothing about business and even less about a used clothing store. That had never stopped me before, so I went down to the Navy Credit Union and applied for a loan. I was nineteen years old with no credit rating to speak of, but unbelievably, they loaned me the money to start my business. We went out and bought thousands of pieces of clothing, racks, and store fixtures. We were ready to make a killing. Of course there is much more to opening a business than buying inventory. We needed a building, utilities, licenses, and all sorts of other stuff we didn't anticipate. We wound up with lots of used clothes and no workable plan to sell them. In the end, we just gave them away and ate the loss. I gave up on the business plan and decided to focus more on my regular job.

One day some lieutenant junior grade staff officer called me and told me to stop by his office. I had no idea who this guy was or why he wanted to see me. Most of the officers in the squadron were pilots, and most had other duties when they weren't flying. This particular officer turned out to be the squadron education officer. This was an additional duty that I am sure wasn't the most glamorous job to have and one that was way under most of the command group's radar. Whoever was unlucky enough to draw the assignment could have easily sat there and accomplished nothing. This officer seemed to care, however, and had actually looked at my personnel file.

I went to his office, and he told me he found I had not graduated from high school. I told him that was correct and that I had quit in the tenth grade. He asked if I had ever considered taking the GED test. I told him no and that I didn't even know what that was. He explained the test to me and told me he had scheduled an appointment for me to take it in a couple of weeks. It still didn't register exactly what was happening, but I went along with the plan. I didn't have any study material and did not take a prep class. I went into the testing facility totally blind, took the test, and waited. I was told when I finished that it would be five to six weeks or more before I knew. I put the test out of my mind, thinking that I had probably failed it anyway.

Several weeks went by, and one day I got a letter in the mail from the Alabama Department of Education. It was my high school equivalency certificate. I had passed the GED on the first try and was now a high school graduate. I would have never taken the test without the insistence of LTJG Lawrence. If he had not cared enough to do his job, I would not be where I am today. I would not have gone to college and certainly would not have been able to experience all that I have in life. I unfortunately lost touch with him shortly after taking the test, and he never knew the impact that he had on my life.

Shortly after receiving the good news from Alabama, I got word that the squadron was indeed deploying for service in Vietnam. We were not actually going to be on the ground in Vietnam; we were going to support the effort there. We were going to the Philippine Islands (PI) and to a navy base called Sangley Point. As the time neared for departure, I applied for leave to take my wife back to Alabama and get ready for the deployment. Back then, the process was to fill out a "leave chit," which was a request form. On the form you asked for the number of days you needed and listed other data, such as contact information. The chit was then run through the chain of command for approval. I requested fifteen days of leave and sent the request through all the proper channels. On the day we were to leave, I stopped by the personnel office and picked up my leave orders. On the bottom of the leave orders was a line for a signature, indicating you received your orders, read them completely, and signed them, agreeing to comply. I signed the document but unfortunately, I did not read it. I was in a hurry and just threw the paper in the car and took off.

We made it back to Alabama and were having a great time. But on about the eighth day of leave, I decided to take a look at the orders to determine what time I was supposed to return. Alas, the orders stated I was approved for six days of leave, which meant I was already AWOL. *There must be some mistake,* I thought, and I immediately called the squadron duty officer. I explained my situation to him, and he could only tell me to get back to the squadron immediately. I jumped in the car and drove like hell back to Jacksonville and turned myself in to the duty officer.

Charges were brought against me for being AWOL, and I went before a captain's mast. Captain's mast in the navy is the lowest rung of the judicial system and is called nonjudicial punishment. It is not a court of record but is a way for a commander to discipline sailors who have committed infractions that do not merit a court-martial. On the day of my mast, the commander of the squadron was on leave, and the executive officer was in temporary command. He used me to make a statement that while he was in command, punishment was going to be harsh. This was way before the 1969 Omnibus Crime Act that, among other things, overhauled the military judicial system, and I wasn't afforded the benefit of counsel. I wasn't allowed to call witnesses or evidence, and it was basically their word against mine. Guess who lost.

Now I wasn't necessarily a model sailor by any stretch of the imagination. I had been in my share of trouble, but this was an error made by some clerk. There was no intent to be AWOL, and I would not have been had I read the orders before I left. The clerk who typed the orders admitted to me that he made a mistake in entering the number of days leave that was approved, but I could not call him as a witness. When this travesty of justice was over, the acting commander reduced me to E1, took away all pay and allowances for three months, placed me on probation for three months, and put me on restriction for three months. I was absolutely devastated. I was being destroyed for something that I really didn't do. Out of the kindness of his heart (or maybe it was guilt), the acting commander did allow me two days to go home and return my car. He took away everything that I had in a matter of minutes. What little career I had was certainly gone now, and the only thing going forward was being away from my wife for a very long time. Needless to say, my morale and attitude went into the toilet and most likely wasn't going to come out for a long time.

The day we were going to leave came quickly. We made our last calls home and boarded a C-141 bound for the PI. This was a long, tortuous flight with very little comfort, and we spent most of our time playing cards. I got into a big game along the way and came out a winner. I won $80 from this guy. But after the game, he said that he couldn't pay me, but he had a nice rifle back home that he would give me for the debt just as soon as we returned to the States. I had been to his house before and saw the gun. I knew that it was worth a lot more than $80, so I agreed.

After more than twenty-four hours on the plane, we finally landed in the PI. We were given a couple of days to get squared away. During that time, I was informed that I was being assigned to the galley. The galley is a mess hall or dining facility, where all the meals are prepared and served. Being sent to the galley was just another way to rub it in further and take me down lower. I thought, *what more can happen to me? There is no more money to take away. I have been reduced to the lowest rank, and now they are sending me to the mess hall to wash dishes.* I made up my mind right then that I'd had enough. I wasn't going to do anything anymore. What could they do to me? If they court-martialed me and sent me to the brig, at least it would be in the States and better than this.

When the day came to report for work, I went in, got a cup of coffee, and sat down at one of the tables. Some guy came over to tell me to get up and go to work. I told him I had no intention of doing anything but sit and drink my coffee. I did this for several days, going through the same routine every day. I came in, got coffee, and sat down while everyone else scurried around, doing their jobs.

One day the supervisor of the dining facility came over and asked if he could sit down with me. I said, "Sure, have a seat." He introduced himself as Petty Officer First Class Rufus L. Baker. He asked me if I wasn't getting tired of just sitting out there by myself. He said he understood why I felt like I did, but I couldn't keep sitting there all day, doing nothing. He said, "If you will work for me and stay out of trouble, I will take care of you. I will do everything I can to help you get back on your feet." Well the truth was that I was kind of getting tired of just sitting, so I took him up on his offer and went to work.

Rufus became my father figure. He listened, and true to his word, he took care of me. He provided gentle guidance and was genuinely concerned about me. I worked hard for Rufus but enjoyed every minute of it because he really cared. The most important thing about Rufus was that he was a teacher. He took me under his wing and taught me how to cook. I went from washing pots and pans or mopping to preparing meals for the squadron. He patiently taught me to read a menu card and calculate recipes. Over the year-long deployment, I prepared everything from soup to lobster and even learned a little about presentation. Military dining facilities have to be spotless, as an outbreak of some food-related illness could render a unit totally ineffective. Rufus was exceptional in his demand for cleanliness. Everything was done a certain way, and there were no substitutes or shortcuts.

About three months into the deployment, I received a call from the personnel office that I had come out on the E-5 promotion list. A couple of months prior to my captains mast, I had taken the promotion test for the next rank and passed, but my score was not high enough to be promoted. I was placed on the stand-by list in case someone was deemed ineligible, for whatever reason, to be promoted. So there I was. Something happened, and I made the promotion list. But I was only an E1, and it's hard to jump all the way to E5. Rufus tried awfully hard to get me reinstated, but in the end, it was just too much to ask, and I had to let the promotion go.

I cannot adequately describe exactly what Rufus meant to me. For the first time in my life, I really felt like I had a purpose and someone who cared about me. Over the years, I applied Rufus's lessons to many aspects of my life. Many years after I was discharged from the navy, I tracked Rufus down and found that he was living down in south Georgia. I went to see him, but I am not sure he knew who I was due to his age and what seemed like the onset of dementia.

CHAPTER 18

A Different Kind of Business

Right before the squadron left Jacksonville for the PI, I had to spend a couple of nights in the barracks. Someone broke into a cigarette machine out in the hall and took all the packs of cigarettes except the Salem brand. They had stacked the packs of Salem cigarettes by the machine and left them. They stayed there until we were getting ready to go to the flight line to board. So as we were leaving, I picked them up and put them in my bag. I figured if someone had not taken care of them by now, they must not want them at all, so why not take them? I didn't smoke this brand, but I hated to just leave them there.

I kept the cigarettes in my bags until long after we arrived in the PI. I had them just lying in my locker, and one day someone mentioned that I could sell them on the black market. I asked around and discovered that was true. For some reason, Filipinos loved Salem cigarettes. You could not give away other brands, but you could sell Salems and make a nice profit. At the time, cigarettes sold in the exchange for $1.10 a carton. You could get $5 a carton outside the gate.

There were a couple of problems, though. First, each service member could only purchase seven cartons per month. Individuals were issued a ration card for cigarettes and liquor every month just to make sure they weren't buying and selling. I suppose this could have upset the balance of the economy or something, but it seemed pretty stupid to me. We have Salems, and they want them and are willing to pay. Why not sell them? So I started a business. I quit smoking myself, which freed up my ration card. But that was only seven cartons. I needed more, and I needed a steady supply. I started researching the members of the squadron to determine who smoked and who didn't. I made a list of those who didn't smoke and then identified those that I thought would go along with giving me their ration cards. There was no name associated with the card, so it didn't matter who used it. Then I went to each one on my list and approached them with the idea of giving the card to me. Some went along right away, figuring they weren't going to use it, so why not give it to me. Others caught on to my plan and wanted a piece of the action for themselves. They agreed to sell me their cards for a set price. I could buy the card and still make money off the cigarettes.

The next problem was getting the cigarettes off base. Guards at the gates had strict orders to search anyone leaving the facility, and if they caught you with cigarettes, it was a court-martial offense. The one exception to that rule were Filipino natives in the US Navy. They were allowed to carry as many cigarettes across as they pleased, unchecked. I cut a deal with a cook in our facility, who agreed to buy them from me at a reduced price. He could then take them across and sell them himself for a profit. It was a great arrangement. He made money, and so did I. As long as no one got greedy, we could all profit. I figured it was justice, since everything had been taken away from me for no good reason. I was simply getting some of it back.

Everything I know about business I learned from this little operation. I learned about supply and demand, inventory, profit and loss, negotiation, and a host of other valuable business lessons. I kept books on the operation because as it grew, there were several other individuals involved. I needed to keep up with who had what and who owed me. A common practice in the navy at the time was what is known as a slush fund. A slush fund is basically a payday lending operation. Someone needs cash to get them through to payday, and he borrows it from you. You charge interest, which at the time was $5 for $7. This meant you loaned someone $5.00, and the borrower paid you back $7 on payday. Many guys made a lot of money this way, but I found a new twist.

I loaned a guy money in exchange for his ration card. I would loan up to $20 for the card. He got the loan and didn't have to pay interest. I got the card, which he wasn't going to use anyway. By the time that we were about three-fourths into the deployment, I was making money hand over fist. I was having a ball, and for the first time in my life, I had money to spend. I went to the enlisted club every Friday night and ate a five-course meal with wine. I got massages at the spa. I started buying custom-made clothes in preparation for returning to the States and getting out.

Life was going great, until one day all hell broke loose. I had a stash of cigarettes ready to go to town, and my regular Filipino guy was off. I badly needed someone to make the trip across, and this guy in the mess hall told me he had a contact on the gate and goes across all the time with stuff. I had an itch that all was not right, but I did the deal with him anyway. He took ten cartons of cigarettes and tried to go across. But his guy was not there, and he got caught with about thirty cartons. Instead of taking ownership of all the cigarettes, he ratted out all of us.

The next thing I knew I was in the Criminal Investigations Office, being questioned about the black marketing. I remembered the last time I was questioned by the authorities, and this time I was prepared. I demanded to talk to a lawyer. They stopped questioning me and sent me over to the Judge Advocate General's office, where I spoke to a navy attorney. He took charge and told me not to worry, that he would take care of everything. I don't know what he did, but he took care of it, as I never heard another word from anyone. Within a couple of weeks, we were redeployed back to the States, and I put my cigarette business behind me for good.

By the time I returned from deployment, I was getting short on cash and only had a few months left in the navy. My wife was settled in Alabama, so I didn't want to move back to Jacksonville. I went home every weekend I was off and many times pushed the envelope as far as I could. I had managed to regain a couple of ranks and was back to E3, but money was still tight. Many weekends I wound up hitchhiking home and back. I must say I had some wild and interesting experiences along the way.

One night I was on my way back to Jacksonville and had caught a ride all the way to Atlanta. That ride let me out at the edge of town, and I was hitching down through the middle of town on Interstate 75, when a guy in a little blue Mustang pulled up and yelled for me to hurry and get in. I noticed immediately that he was a shady-looking character. Something told me this wasn't going down right. He peeled away and was flying through Atlanta. He was nervous and constantly looking around, but after a while, started to settle down some. He later told me he had robbed a liquor store right before he stopped for me. He said the cops would be looking for a single guy, and with me in the car, they wouldn't be suspicious and would pass on by. He told me all the details of the robbery and how it went down, until we got well on the south side of Atlanta. He pulled up to a side street and told me I should get out. I quickly got out of the car, and he sped off down the side street. I guess all things considered, it worked out okay. He got what he needed, and so did I. I was relieved to get out of that car, though.

Another time I was hitching from Jacksonville to Alabama on Interstate 75 North when a big, old, long Lincoln pulled up. There were three black people inside, two black males and a black female. They had all been drinking heavily and were trashed. I got into the backseat with one of the guys, who was waving a bottle around and passing it between the front and back. He offered me a drink, which I quickly declined. They were laughing and cussing each other, when the guy in the backseat got mad at the driver and pulled out a pistol. He waved it around, yelling at the driver and telling him that he was going to kill him. The girl in the front passenger seat started screaming and begging him to put away the gun. Everybody was ignoring me, and I really think they had forgotten that I was in the car. I had to think fast and get out of that car as soon as possible. I picked a time when the guy in the back seemed to calm down a little, and I told the driver I would get out at the next intersection. They had forgotten where I had told them I was going, so the driver pulled over and let me out. They were still raising hell when they pulled away and headed down the highway. Of all the people going toward Alabama that I could have gotten a ride from, I had to wind up with those idiots.

On another trip home, I got a ride with an old, burly truck driver. He was a bear of a man with all the personality to go with it. He made me laugh all the way to Rome, Georgia. But before we got there, he told me that he needed to make a stop just outside of Cartersville if I didn't mind. Well when you are riding with someone else and it's cold outside, you don't mind what the person does as long as the vehicle is going in the right direction. So I didn't ask what he needed to do; I just went along. We drove down this long, winding driveway just outside of town and soon pulled up to this big, old house. He climbed out of the truck and said he would be right back. He was gone maybe thirty minutes and climbed back up in the truck. He told me that he had a date. What it really turned out to be was a trip to a cathouse. Hey, who am I to judge? As soon as his date was over, he drove me on to Rome, which was only forty miles or so from home, and I was a happy camper.

In all the years of hitchhiking, I never felt in any real danger. Nor was I ever really scared. Now being in the car with a bunch of drunks who are waving guns around is not the safest thing I ever did, but I still wasn't scared enough to stop hitching. I have had folks wreck their cars trying to stop for me. And one time, I had somebody throw eggs at me while I was standing on the road hitching, but overall, it was just a cheap way to travel.

There were times when I had just enough money to drive home and back. On one of those nights, I was driving north up Interstate 75 at about seventy-five miles an hour. Back then, the speed limit changed from day to night. It was seventy-five during the day but dropped to sixty-five at night. So I was speeding! All of a sudden I looked in my mirror, and there were blue lights flashing behind me. I was being pulled over. A big, mean-looking Georgia state trooper informed me that I was doing ten miles over the speed limit, and he was giving me a ticket, for which I would have to post a cash bond. The bond was about $28, but it might as well have been $3,000, for I only had a couple of dollars and a pack of cigarettes to my name. He told me that if I couldn't post bond, I would have to go to jail. Well I had no choice but jail, so I followed him down some back roads to this little town, and he pulled up in front of the jail.

The sheriff lived at the jail in an apartment, so the trooper knocked on the door and woke him up. He came to the door in a pair of overalls, no shoes and no shirt. The trooper told him that he had one for him and gave him the details of my horrendous crime. The sheriff told me to get on upstairs and that he wanted to go back to bed. I asked him if I could make my one phone call. He said yes, but only one.

The problem was we didn't have a phone at home, and I didn't have any idea who to call. I did know that I didn't want to spend any more time in this filthy jail than I had to. So I thought fast. My wife's uncle had a phone, and I just happened to know the number. Unfortunately, the uncle was stone deaf. When he answered the phone, I knew that I was in trouble. I had to tell him three or four times to please go get my wife and tell her to come to the jail and get me out. He also had to tell her that she had to bring cash to post my bond and how much. We went back and forth for several minutes, and all the while, the sheriff was getting madder and madder. He kept telling me to hang up and get into the cell so he could go back to sleep. Finally, he just hung up the phone for me and told me to get in the cell.

I have never been in a filthier place in all of my life. The mattresses on the bunks were greasy and dusty, and the whole place stunk. There were several other guys in the cell with me, and they did not appreciate being awakened, either. I managed to hold them off by giving away my cigarettes. Then I made a hammock out of one of the cleaner bedsheets tied to two steam pipes.

The next day, my wife finally showed up with the bond money, and I was freed. I had spent over seven hours in that jail, but it seemed like a lifetime. The hardest part of the night was not knowing if she had gotten the right location or if she could find the place even if her uncle managed to tell her right. I didn't know if she had any money or where she could get some. It all worked out in the end, and I learned one thing that night; I don't ever want to be in jail. The loudest noise that I have ever heard was those cell doors closing.

When we got back from that deployment, I went to collect on the poker game from the trip over, but the guy had some bad news. When he got home, he found out that his wife had left him and taken everything he owned. She had sold everything, so there was no way to get anything back. Of course, that meant he didn't have the rifle he promised me. He did make good on the debt, though. There was one thing she didn't know about and didn't take. He bought a motorcycle just before we deployed and had stored it in Jacksonville. He gave me the motorcycle to cover the debt. It was a small bike and fit in the trunk of the old car that I had at the time. That next weekend I planned to take it home to Alabama and leave it until I could figure out what to do with it.

A fellow sailor needed a ride that weekend, so on Friday evening, we loaded up my old car and headed north. We got into Alabama around 2:00 a.m. and had just started over Lookout Mountain when the car ran out of gas. I had hoped we would make it all the way, but we had no such luck. There was no traffic on the road to hitch, so there was only one thing to do. We took the little bike out of the trunk and, after some tinkering, got it fired up. Both of us got on and away we went. The only problem was I had never ridden a motorcycle before and had no idea what to do. I figured that it must be somewhat like riding a bicycle, so with a little effort, we rode that thing off Lookout Mountain and down to my house. Later in the day, my wife and I took some gas to the car on the mountain and then took my friend to his house. I have been riding motorcycles ever since that night, and have owned several, but none as memorable as that little Honda.

CHAPTER 19

New Life

I settled in on the base at Jacksonville and counted the days until discharge. I tried to go back to the base dining facility and work for Rufus, but right before we redeployed home, he was promoted to chief petty officer. As soon as we got back to the States, he was reassigned somewhere else. I really didn't want to work for anyone else, and I was too close to discharge for a real assignment. So I was sent to the supply depot to drive a truck, delivering supplies. It turned out to be a great job. I picked up my truck in the mornings and loaded it with whatever needed delivering. The rest of the day was spent driving from unit to unit.

Within a couple of months after we redeployed, I received word that the president was releasing thousands of soldiers, sailors, and airmen early. I was due to be discharged on the day before my birthday in January, but with this news, I would get out on the 17th of December. That was just over a month away, but to a short-timer it was a lifetime. I was overjoyed. I passed the time driving my truck and trying to stay out of trouble until discharge day finally came. I had spent the better part of the last week clearing the installation, getting records, and turning in equipment. On the final day at NAS Jacksonville, I took all my uniforms and threw them in the hallway. I packed my ditty bag, put on some civilian clothes, and headed for Alabama. Of course, I hitchhiked. I couldn't spend money on plane fare my last day in the navy.

I made it back to Alabama and civilian life. My wife and I had never really lived together as man and wife, other than the short time right before we deployed, so this was going to take some getting used to. The first thing I had to do was find a job. The problem was that nothing much had changed in Fort Payne, and jobs were not to be found. The nearest city that had jobs was Chattanooga, so I started looking there. Every day I picked up a copy of the *Chattanooga Times Free Press* and scanned the want ads.

One day I happened onto what sounded like a dream job. The ad spoke of huge salaries, great working conditions, and promotion opportunities. Just what I was looking for! I thought, *Why start at the bottom when you can start at the top?* So I jumped in our old car and drove to Chattanooga. I checked into a rundown motel close to the address in the ad and went to apply. The job turned out to be in sales and wound up being the biggest scam that I have ever heard of.

The concept worked like this. Several women worked in what was called the phone room, and they went from number to number in the Chattanooga phone book. They called the number, and when the person answered, the women went through a prepared script. They introduced themselves and said they represented a market study firm doing some research in the Chattanooga area. The purpose of the research was to determine the salability of certain products that had just come on the market. They informed the people they called that they had been selected to participate in the research and would receive a nice gift for their trouble. If the conversation got far enough, they would make an appointment to come in, review the products, and pick up their gifts. If an appointment was made, it was forwarded to the sales department, and that was where I came in.

There was a showroom full of items, ranging from a gasoline lawnmower, vacuum cleaner, cookware, and sewing machine to various electric hand-tools and a chainsaw. None of these products were necessarily new or innovative. They were products you could buy anywhere.

Once the people came for their appointment, a salesman took them into a fancy office full of really nice and impressive furniture.

This office was a prop and only used to make sales presentations. None of us had offices, especially not as nice as this one.

We also had a script to follow. We told them how lucky they were to have been selected for this very important market research. We told them a little about our company and why we were conducting the research. After this bit of softening up, we took them into the showroom and went from product to product, explaining everything about each one. We emphasized how a product could change someone's life and make it easier. Each product had a separate script, pointing out certain aspects of its performance. For example, the sewing machine was touted as whisper quiet and especially balanced. We would make a big deal of turning the machine on with something balanced on the top of the machine. Of course, the item didn't fall over, indicating the precision of the construction. Ball bearings were used to demonstrate the suction of the vacuum cleaner, and there was a series of functions we went through to demonstrate the capabilities of the lawnmower.

Throughout the demonstration, we watched the people's reactions to different products. If they paid particular attention to a specific item, we came back to it over and over. We also made mental notes of which products they were interested in. At the end of each demonstration, we gave them a price that was suggested for the sale of the product. These prices were extremely high, but after our demonstration, we had them convinced it was a bargain.

After this song and dance sales demonstration was over, we asked the participants to pick four products they liked best. This was done under the guise that it was part of the market research. When they finished picking out the four products, we sprung the trap. "If I could get you a special deal on those products, would you be interested?" "What kind of special deal?" they would ask. I would tell them to hold on a second, I would call my manager and ask. I faked a phone call supposedly to ask if I could sell them the products. And, of course, the answer was always yes. "Guess what folks! I have just been authorized to sell you those four products for the low, low price of $398. That is $400 off the recommended price! We can do this because we need to build up name recognition in this area and get these products out in the marketplace. So can I have these loaded into your car?"

You would not believe how many people fell for this scam. I sold a package to one woman, and when I was demonstrating the cookware, she said that she liked it. When I asked her what she liked most about it, she replied, "Ooh, I like shiny things." So she took home a carload of shiny things that day. I knew from day one that I was not cut out to be a salesman, and I also knew that even if I was, I didn't want to work a scam like this. I left the company after about a month. My wife had taken a job in the phone room about the same time that I became a salesman and stayed on for several months after I left.

So I was back to looking for a job. By this time, we had completely moved to Chattanooga, so it was going to be there somewhere. I decided to try an employment agency and see what they could find for me. It turned out that my most useful experience from my navy days was as a cook, so naturally they suggested that I should be a restaurant manager. I entered the management training program for Shoney's Restaurant Company. The franchisee for the Chattanooga area had about four or five restaurants close by, so there was room for advancement.

At the time, Shoney's was one of the fastest-growing and most profitable chains in the business. The concept had grown out of the Big Boy franchise. The guy who created the Big Boy sandwich had franchised it and broken the United States into territories. One man created Frisch's Big Boy, and another Bob's Big Boy. The Southeastern district was bought by Alex Schoenbaum, and he called his franchise Shoney's. The concept centered on the sandwich, which was a double-decker similar to the Big Mac. Of course, there were other items on the menu, including steaks and seafood, but the namesake was the Big Boy.

Shoney's had, by far, the best philosophy for running a restaurant that I have ever seen. Everything was step by step, from the cooking of the food to the servers waiting tables. Nothing was left to chance, and there was a procedure for everything. Shoney's also had a first-class management training program. By the time a trainee completed the program, he or she could run any size restaurant anywhere. I started out at the Brainerd Road location, which was probably the busiest of all the locations in the franchise area. Shoney's program was fast-paced, with classroom training coupled with hands-on experience. I learned every aspect of the restaurant operation, from preparing every dish to waiting tables. I did it all. After several weeks, I completed the training course and joined the management team.

Within a month or so, the franchisee opened a new store in Rossville, Georgia, which is just across the line from Chattanooga, and I was reassigned to the new store. To celebrate the grand opening, the entire team of the new store was invited to the owner's home for a grand-opening party. My wife and I loaded up in our old '59 Buick and drove up the mountain to his house. This was no ordinary house. It was a mansion in every sense of the word. The house was huge, and when we rang the doorbell, a uniformed butler answered the door. I have never been inside a more grandiose home. There were uniformed servers carrying trays of drinks and food, and there were bottles and bottles of champagne. At some point in the evening, my wife and a couple other women went into the ladies room. When they came out, they were chattering like mad about the room. They were blown away by the size of it. Many said there was more room in the ladies room than in the entire house they lived in.

When the evening was over, we said our good-byes, thanked the host and hostess, and climbed back in the old Buick for the trip down the mountain and home. We pulled out just ahead of another couple, and they followed us all the way down the mountain. I knew we were low on gas, but I hoped that we would make it home. That was not to be the case, however, and halfway down the mountain the old car coughed and died. There was nowhere to pull off the road, and with the couple right behind us, there was nothing to do but put the car in neutral and coast down the mountain. We would have died of embarrassment to have to stop and admit that we ran out of gas. So we just coasted along until we made it all the way down. Our luck held out, and there was a station at the foot of the mountain. We coasted right up to the pump, and no one ever knew our dilemma.

I was doing fine at Shoney's, but I always felt like something was missing or that I could do more with my life. I started thinking about going into business for myself and began looking around. The problem was that I had no idea what kind of business I was looking for or how to go about finding it. I finally decided on a gas station. Why I made this decision I have no idea, but nothing would do except to find a station and buy it. Where I was going to get the money was a concern that I should have thought of, but it never crossed my mind; I was going to get into the gas station business. That was all I thought about day in and day out. I even made up a business plan, though I didn't know that was what I was doing. I made rules for the way I thought a gas station should be run. I guess that I based this on my own experiences while traveling, but I am not certain. I spent hours each week scanning the want ads in every paper that I could find. I drove into every station that I passed on my way to work just to see how they ran. In other words, I was obsessed. There were a couple of stations listed from time to time, and I spent hours checking them out. But for whatever reason, they didn't work out. They were either too old, in the wrong place, or overpriced.

Then one day out of the blue, I saw exactly what I was looking for: A brand-new Phillips 66 gas station was listed. The station was a company-owned store on a major highway just outside downtown Chattanooga. It was a full-service station with three bays and two sets of pumps. The most significant thing about this particular station was a giant plastic cowboy. The cowboy held a tire in his hand and was used to advertise tires. Over the years, he became an advertising icon. So after doing some due diligence, I contacted the local office of Phillips Petroleum and set up an appointment to discuss the sale.

I was twenty-two years old and in debt with no money. But I pressed forward and went to the appointment. I rattled off some of my proposed rules for running a business and, undoubtedly, made quite an impression because the vice president I spoke with said he was going to do whatever he could to get me in that station. He went so far as to offer me a job running the station until all the financing could be arranged to buy it. The fact he was going to pay me half of what I made at Shoney's never entered my mind. I was sold hook, line, and sinker. I resigned from Shoney's immediately and started off on my new career of gas station manager.

When I took over the station, there were two employees already working there. They had been stealing the company blind and were not too happy to see me come in. In the first place, they could tell right off that I had no clue of what I was doing. And second, they didn't want me messing up their good deal. I charged ahead anyway, determined that I could win them over and make it in the gas business. After a week of putting up with them, I decided it was time to part ways with one of them, so I fired him. He was none too happy with my decision and basically threatened me. I was too young and too stupid to pay a lot of attention to his rantings, and I just let it go. I kept the other guy on, and I think that firing his coworker got his attention somewhat.

After about a week, Phillips called me and told me to meet them at a bank in downtown Chattanooga. I drove over, and we met with a loan officer of the bank. After some preliminary conversation, I left with a note for $40,000. I had no money, no credit, no assets, and no security, but the bank loaned me a small fortune. I don't think I even knew how many zeroes were in that much money. It was certainly more than I had ever dreamed of. Unfortunately, I wasn't really sure what I had borrowed the money for. I had no idea what the inventory was, tools, equipment, or anything. I just signed a bunch of papers.

When I opened up the station as my own business, I had to take my wife's paycheck and put it in the register in order to make change. It seemed like Phillips was taking money from the station every day for one thing or the other. There were weeks that I had to take money from her check just to break even with Phillips.

Within a couple months of taking over the station and borrowing lots of money, Phillips notified me that I had to go to station management school in Memphis, Tennessee. This was a three-week course designed to teach everything one would ever want to know about gasoline and how to sell it. I packed up our old car and headed for Memphis. I checked into an old, rundown hotel, which had a contract with Phillips to house all of us, and began the task of learning about gas.

My wife and I never had any money, and this time was no exception. I had just enough money for gas to get there, and since all our meals were furnished, I really didn't need any. It got a little boring just staying in my room every night, while the other students checked out the nightlife in town. So one night I got into a poker game with some of the guys. I don't remember where I got enough money to stake me in the game, but I had just enough to get into a couple hands. My luck for poker held out, and I wound up winning big before the night was over. When I say big, I mean maybe $25 or so. But that was huge for the time, especially since I was totally broke. That money got me through the course and allowed me to go out at least a couple of times.

The course was interesting but did very little to equip someone to manage a station. It was too in-depth, with a lot of time spent discussing refineries and the process for refining gasoline. The course also spent a lot of time teaching about tires and how they were made, instead of telling you how to sell them. There was very little time spent on teaching accounting measures or business practices, both of which would have been a welcome subject for me.

I completed the course and made my way back to Chattanooga. Before I left, I had pulled the old Buick into one of the bays and locked it up. The engine had some problem, and I didn't have time to fix it before I left. I had just put four new tires on the old car. When I got back from the school, I found the car out in the parking lot, with all the tires gone. The car was sitting on the ground beside the station. When I drove up and saw it, I just lost it. Someone from Phillips had told the guy I left in charge to pull the car out and leave it. Of course, it became an attractive target for some thieves, and they took advantage of it. I strongly suspect the guy I fired was involved. I called him on it and went right to the edge of accusing him, but he denied any involvement. I put two old recaps on the Buick and had it towed to a salvage yard and sold it.

I lost all respect for Phillips after that, and the relationship continued to go downhill. After about six months of running the station and not making a dime, I started looking around for something else. Phillips and I had several yelling matches, and it was becoming obvious that the deck was being stacked against me.

Around that time, my wife's sister and her husband moved from Alabama to Cleveland, Tennessee, where he had taken a job running a body shop. He and some partners were renting the shop from a guy who was doing time in federal prison for interstate auto theft. It seems that he found out he could make much more money from stealing and stripping cars than he could by repairing them. The property the shop was on totaled over twenty acres and was way out in the country, which made for a perfect hiding place for stolen cars. Unfortunately, he got greedy and careless, and the feds soon came down on him. He was sent to federal prison in Atlanta, and his wife maintained the property while he was gone.

My brother-in-law arranged for me to work in the shop with him, and my wife and I decided to move. I had bought an old Ford for road service. The old car ran okay and had four nearly new tires on it. I went down to the station, took all the money out of the register, took any tools that were mine, and pulled the old Ford right up to the front door. I jacked it up, took all four tires off, let it down right there in the doorway, and drove off. I never looked back, and I never heard from Phillips after that.

We moved into a tiny apartment in Cleveland, and I went to work in the body shop. I knew less about body work than I did about running a gas station, but it was a job. So we settled in. I did mostly grunt work in the shop and left the complex stuff to my brother-in-law. He taught me to sand, tape, and prep cars for painting as well as simple tasks, such as putting on replacement parts. The shop eventually fell on hard times and wasn't making a lot of money. I stayed with him as long as I could, but it was becoming obvious that he couldn't afford to keep me. So I started looking around for a job again.

I answered an ad from the local Ford dealer in Cleveland, who wanted a body man for their shop. I was honest up front and told them my limitations, but they took a chance and hired me anyway. I was beginning to like the body shop trade and made up my mind I was going to teach myself everything there was to know about it. When I went to work at the Ford shop, I did the same things that I had been doing before: taping and sanding.

On my lunch break, I started taking old, bent-up fenders and other parts and practicing repairing them. I pulled out dents, ground them down, and put on a coat of primer all on my own time. I also started learning how to mix and spray paint. The shop foreman took notice of my efforts and let me prep cars for painting. That meant I primed cars for the painter as well as other tasks beyond just taping them out. I quickly got to the point where he let me spray small jobs, such as fenders or hoods, that didn't require a lot of expertise.

One day it happened. He asked me to paint an entire car. The car was a fairly new, light-yellow Plymouth. I did all the body work, prep, primer, and taping. I mixed the paint and shot the car all by myself. The paint job was flawless, and I was extremely proud of my efforts. From that day forward, I was considered a body man and took on almost any job in the shop.

My old business instincts started up again, and I saw an opportunity. The shop didn't like to work on anything but Fords, unless the dealer owned the car, as was the case with the Plymouth. If a customer came for an estimate on anything but a Ford, the foreman estimated the repair but told the customer he or she would have to go elsewhere to get it fixed. I saw this as a business opportunity and started buying up body shop equipment slowly but steadily. I bought an air compressor, paint gun, hoses, and body-working tools. As soon as I acquired enough to do most body work, I went into action. I watched for a customer to come in driving something besides a Ford to get an estimate. I looked for small jobs that would not require anything but a small repair and repaint. When they left, I got a copy of the estimate. I took the phone number from the estimate, called them up, and offered to repair the car. I told the potential customer I would repair it much cheaper than the estimate, and they could keep the extra money from their insurance. And I guaranteed my work. Surprisingly, most people took me up on my offer.

I started making money right away. I had the customer bring the car to my little apartment and leave it until I could get it repaired. I did all the work in my driveway after I got home from work. Most nights I was out there, working on a car until after midnight. I got up the next morning and either took the car to work or made arrangements for the customer to pick it up at my house. Everything was cash and immediate. I had an account with a parts company but paid in cash when I could. I put everything I made right back into the business and was building up quite a shop. I started looking around for a building to move into and started thinking about going into business full time. I found an old garage that could be rented, moved all my equipment in, and set up a business. I worked out of the building for several weeks with the same arrangement as before, until I was satisfied that I could make it. Then I quit the job at the dealership.

At the time, Cleveland was known worldwide as the "used car capitol of the world," and there were hundreds of car dealers operating there. The scam was that they would go up north to somewhere like Detroit, Michigan, or Cleveland, Ohio, and buy cars that had rusted out from the snow and ice. They transported them to Cleveland, Tennessee, made the necessary repairs, and either sold the cars there or, in some cases, transported them back and sold them as a "Southern car."

Most of the repairs consisted of grinding out all of the rust and repairing it with Bondo, a plastic-like material that bonds to metal quite well. It can be sanded easily and is very easy to work with. Some of the more drastic cars needed some sort of filler to hold the Bondo in place. I developed a trick of taking thin screen wire and forming it to the area in need of repair. I then built up the area with Bondo, until I got it to the point where I could sand it down for painting. I used masking tape as well, even though it is certainly not as strong as wire.

Most of the dealers involved in this trade were unscrupulous at best and only wanted cars fixed as cheaply as possible. They didn't care about long-term repairs, just enough to get it sold. I obliged them as much as possible. I used to joke that if you brought me two bumpers and told me what color you wanted, I would build you a car. I hooked up with one dealer who had a reputation for all sorts of dirty dealing. His biggest claim to fame was turning back odometers. He would take in a car with, say, 100,000 miles on it, and after I finished my magic repair job, would turn the odometer back to, say, 60,000 miles. A quick trip over the line into Alabama for a title, and you had a low-mileage, clean, Southern car that had never seen snow or ice. Of course, a quick scan with a magnet would easily find all the repair work, but most people didn't bother. I was turning over six or seven cars a day in my shop, working alone.

I soon hired a guy to do the grunt work who worked with me at the Ford dealership. He was also one of the best "wheel" men I have ever seen. Back then, we painted everything with either enamel or lacquer. Enamel is very difficult to use, and I avoided it at all costs, which meant I painted everything with lacquer. Once a lacquer paint job is finished and allowed to dry, it has to be wheeled out and polished. It takes a steady hand to do a good polish job because it is easy to burn the paint, particularly on the edges, and he was one of the best.

When we got married, my wife had really crooked teeth in the front. It bothered her tremendously, even though it didn't bother me. She really wanted to get them straightened. She never asked for much, so I was determined to get them fixed for her. I talked her into going to a dentist. He told her that he could pull them all and replace them with a partial in front. Today this would have never happened because of new methods. But back then, it was all she had to choose from, so she did it. She was worried to death about how we were going to pay the bill, but I told her not to worry, that I would get the money. The bill came to around $500. I went to work, calling some of the dealers in the area to get some cars to work on. I did not leave the shop until I had made enough money to pay her dental bill. I stayed there all night and part of the next day, but when I came out, it was paid in full. She got her new partial, and it changed her life forever. She actually smiled, something she hardly ever did before.

We were cooking along and making fairly good money, mostly from the crooked dealer. One day he brought me an old Fairlane. This car had one of the worst paint jobs on it that I had ever seen. There was some minor damage to the car he wanted fixed that would result in a fairly small paint job. I told him as soon as I saw it that the paint would never match and would look like crap, but he wanted it done anyway. We took in the car and made the repairs. After the paint dried, it looked bad. My paint was all shiny and new-looking. It stood out from the rest of the car. I took the car to him and gave him my bill. He went out, looked at the car, and sure enough, raised hell about the paint job. He yelled about me guaranteeing my work and that this was unsatisfactory. I told him I did guarantee my work, and yes, I would fix it. I took the car back to the shop and told my hired hand to strip it down to the metal. I left him to that task and went home for a short while. When I came back, he had done as I asked, and the car was shining like a nickel. I spent the rest of the night building the paint back up. I reprimed it, and when the primer dried, I painted the entire car from top to bottom. When I finished, I had my hired hand wheel the car out and then we waxed it. It was basically a new car when we finished. The work we did would have cost the dealer ten times what I charged him for the small repair he originally wanted. But I had guaranteed my work. I took the car back to him and let him look at it. Of course, he was overjoyed at the results and gladly paid me the small amount for the original repair. I told him to enjoy the car because that was the last one I would ever fix for him.

I went back to the shop and started loading up all my equipment. I closed the shop and never worked for a used car dealer again. I returned to the Ford dealership and soon found a new way to make money. I was still repairing cars in my driveway and found out one day that the dealership often sold vehicles they had towed and stored at the facility. When the owner failed to claim the cars, they could be sold, and most were auctioned off. The dealer offered to sell them to me if I took all of them and could get them off the property. I readily agreed and partnered with a coworker to make the purchase. We bought eleven cars the first time and continued to buy the cars for several months afterward. We moved the cars to some property that he owned and either repaired them or stripped them for parts.

One day out of the blue, I got a call from the guy who owned the body shop where my brother-in-law had worked. This was the fellow who had done time for auto theft. After his time was up, he came back to Cleveland to take over the shop. I had met him a couple of times, and on one occasion, he let me see a guitar he bought while in prison.

It was a gorgeous Gibson flat-top box and was much more guitar than I could ever afford. I admired it and even played it some. I jokingly told him to let me know if he ever wanted to sell it. I was shocked beyond belief when I answered his call and heard him ask if I really wanted to buy the guitar. Of course I wanted to buy it. The real question was for how much. I expected him to say some figure that was way beyond my means and couldn't believe it when he said he needed money and would sell it to me for $150. That was a fourth of what the Gibson was worth, and, of course, I told him I would take it. I made arrangements to pick up the guitar later in the evening.

The only problem was I didn't have any money. So I immediately went into super-salesman mode. I called everyone that I had done business with and told them I was having a "fire sale" in used cars. I sold four or five cars by the end of the day and had enough money to go get the Gibson. The guitar was, and still is, my pride and joy. Over the years before the army, I pawned it at least a hundred times. I always got it out and never came close to losing it, even though the pawnbroker hoped I would.

I eventually left the body shop and went back into the restaurant business. I bounced around from one to the other for about a year, but nothing seemed to be what I was looking for. A friend came by one day and told me about a big airplane plant near Atlanta that had just gotten a big government contract. He said they were hiring and paid really good money, and he wanted to go down and apply. He invited me to go along, and I agreed. I thought, *What the heck? Anything beats the restaurant business.* We got to the Lockheed Aircraft plant, filled out applications, and much to our surprise, were hired on the spot. My friend had some experience working on airplanes while in the air force, but my only experience was fueling them while on the ship. At any rate, they hired both of us and gave me a starting wage that was more money than I had ever dreamed of making. Lockheed was a union plant and with this big contract to build the C-5, was offering huge money to work there.

I left my wife back in Tennessee and moved in with her aunt Bertha and uncle Houston, who lived about twenty miles from the plant. I had never met them, but they took me right in and made me feel at home. Aunt Bertha was a special person, as was her husband, Houston. They lived on a small farm and grew massive gardens. Bertha was one of the best cooks I have ever known and always fixed huge meals. For the first month, I worked the night shift and didn't get home until after 11:00 most nights. They would have gone to bed long before, but Bertha always had my supper waiting on the stove. They never asked for money or hinted that I wasn't welcome. They were the kindest people I have met in my entire life. They never complained about anything, and I never heard a cross word between them in the month I lived there.

    I eventually transferred to days, and my wife and I found a small apartment close to where my friend who went with me to Lockheed lived. It was a good distance from the plant, but I didn't know where else to move, so we went where he was. On the day we moved, we loaded everything we owned into a Ryder rental truck and started for Georgia. I had driven a truck while in the navy, so this was no big deal, just drive and get there as soon as possible. We made it about a mile from our house and had to go under a railroad overpass. Just as I started to drive under the bridge, I saw a sign that said, "Warning low overhead." At the same time, I realized the truck was taller than the bridge, but it was too late. We hit that bridge and tore the entire top off the truck. Just peeled that sucker back like a can of sardines. We finally got the truck out of the bridge and were on our way. The problem was the whole top was gone from the truck. We followed a rain cloud the entire way to Georgia and sweated that it would start raining before we got there. When we did finally make to my friend's house, I realized I couldn't leave the truck parked outside because if it rained, all our stuff would be ruined. My friend and I drove around the area until we found a barn that had an opening big enough to park the truck in. We pulled the truck in and left it for the night. The next day we went back and recovered the truck, and I doubt the owner of the property even knew we had been there.

    My wife and I settled into our apartment, and I started building airplanes, or at least that was what I thought I was going to do.

Lockheed was a union plant, and the union controlled everything. The one thing I learned in this whole experience was that I never want to work in a union environment ever again. This particular union wanted to drag this contract out as long as it could and get the maximum overtime at the same time. In other words, we weren't allowed to work. Now that seems a little dramatic, but it is the gospel truth. When we clocked in at the beginning of our shifts, the union supervisor told us to just stay out of sight. Don't do anything, but don't get caught. When the shift ended, the same supervisor told us overtime was needed, and he needed as many of us to stay as possible. Then it was the same thing all over again; stay out of sight, and don't do anything.

The problem was how to stay out of sight for eight hours and not be seen by management. I developed a scam that ensured I didn't do any work but gave the appearance I did. I learned quickly inspectors went from job to job, checking the work to ensure it met all safety requirements. These guys wore hard hats, carried clipboards and flashlights, and walked from area to area. Sounded like the perfect plan to me. So I found a hard hat, clipboard, and flashlight and went to work. The Lockheed plant is one mile long and one mile wide. At the time, it was the largest building in the world without a partition or wall inside, and it would take several hours to walk around. I walked around and around the building with my clipboard and stopped now and then, looking like I knew what I was doing. I shined my light up into some part of the airplane and then moved on somewhere else. I did this for several weeks, and no one ever challenged me or asked me what I was doing.

Unfortunately, all good things must end, and Lockheed was no exception. The union almost bankrupted the plant with its shenanigans, and the federal government had to bail out the company. One of the requirements for the loan was a tightening of expenses, which meant layoffs for some employees, and the rest had to really go to work. The plant rounded up all the employees who had not reached the magic ninety-day period that would trigger recall rights and issued layoff notices. I had been at Lockheed eighty-eight days, so guess who got a slip. Yep, time to move on once again. Like the Beverly Hillbillies, we loaded our truck and moved to Tennessee.

By this time, I had probably held twenty jobs. I had been a truck driver, restaurant manager, cook, body man, service station owner, and aircraft builder. I had sold insurance and had run a debit route. Now I was unemployed once again, only this time there was a new twist. My wife was pregnant with our first child. We had been married for five years and been trying to have a baby the entire time. We had just about given up hope of her ever getting pregnant. Every month it was up and down. She would be late and get all excited, until she went to the doctor. Then it would be down again when she found out she wasn't pregnant. But dreams do come true, and finally, one day she found out she was, in fact, pregnant.

She found out while we were still at Lockheed. As soon as we moved back to Tennessee, she went to a doctor there. The doctor she picked was a real old, country doctor. The first time he saw her, he came into the exam room and said to her, "Girl, there ain't much to you, is there?" I guess he was referring to the fact she probably didn't weigh more than one hundred pounds, even pregnant. I should have made her go to another doctor after that, but she wanted to stay with him. There was joy in our household, and I didn't have to go through the ups and downs of wanting to be pregnant.

I guess every expectant mother goes through all sorts of quirky eating habits. Some want ice cream and pickles, while others may go crazy wanting peanut butter. My wife craved raw oysters and raw potatoes. Her cravings were so strong that on occasion, we would be driving down the road, and she would suddenly yell out, "Stop the car!" I would pull into the parking lot of a grocery store, and she would be getting out of the car even before it stopped. She tore into the store like a mad person until she found oysters and a bag of potatoes. Then she came back to the car and started eating them right there in the parking lot. This was a person who had never eaten an oyster in her life and did not like anything slimy even touching her. So this craving was exceptionally strong.

We finally made it back to Tennessee and found an apartment. I went back to my brother-in-law's shop for a few weeks, until I could find something else to do. I started taking stock of my life and began to realize I was going nowhere fast. I began to think about going to college. Uncle Jack had graduated from the University of Alabama, and that was an inspiration. I thought, *If he could do it, so can I.* The problem was that I had no idea of how to start looking, much less going. There was a small community college in Cleveland, and I inquired there. I decided that I might want to be a computer programmer because that seemed to be the best-paying job at the time. Computers were just starting to make headlines, and programming was the rage. I checked into the college's programming degree and actually started the enrollment process. I never bothered to find out if I had the aptitude for such a program; I just went ahead with it. I had a full GI bill, but I knew I needed a suitable job to supplement what I would get.

I looked around for something with very little stress that would be steady. A local fast-food restaurant was looking for a grill cook. I had made it through Shoney's management program and had worked at a couple of restaurants, so I figured being a grill cook wouldn't be too bad. I applied, was hired right away, and started to work immediately. No sooner had I started than I realized that the restaurant was a disaster. It was doing a good business but was poorly managed. The owner of the store was a franchiser and had several other stores. He had entered into a partnership with a guy to be the general manager over all of them. The general manager had the personality of a bull and knew very little about the restaurant business. He was gruff and very blunt with employees and customers alike. The store manager of the store where I worked was a complete idiot and a yes-man for him. The other employees came and went as they pleased, and it was obvious there was considerable stealing going on. But I figured, *What the heck? I am just the grill cook, and it's none of my affair to deal with.* I went to work and did my job for several weeks, still finishing up the application process for college. I didn't want to take on any other responsibilities and had no intention of trying to straighten anything out. I just wanted to work and get on with my life.

Things were going pretty well, and I was tolerating the inefficiency until one day after a huge lunch rush. I asked one of the cashiers to help me clean up and restock. I thought it was a reasonable request, and she didn't object. I wasn't trying to take over the store; I was just using the Rufus concept of "If you got time to lean, you got time to clean." The manager heard me ask her to help and went ballistic. He yelled at me, telling me I was just the cook and that he was the manager. If there were to be any orders given, he would be the one doing it. I replied, "Okay, that's enough for me. I am out of here." I was not going to work in a place so poorly managed any longer. I took off my apron, threw it in the floor, and headed for the door.

As I was going out, the owner of the store was coming in. He saw I was leaving and asked what was going on. I told him I had quit and that he could have his restaurant and the manager, too. He said, "Hey, slow down, take it easy, and just tell me what happened." He asked me to step outside with him, and we talked. I laid it all out for him, including what was wrong with the store. I told him he was being robbed blind and that the manager was a nut. When I finished ranting, he said, "Stay right here, and don't go anywhere."

He went inside and was gone for a few minutes. When he came back out, the manager was with him. The manager kept walking to his car and left. The owner asked if I would manage the store for him. He said he had known for some time there were problems but never knew for sure what they were. I was shocked. I wasn't ready for this and had plans to go to college. I told him this, but he insisted and told me if I got the store straightened out, he would make sure that I could do both. I reluctantly agreed, and he assured me that I had his full backing, even with the general manager. The first thing I did was fire the cook, who I knew had been stealing box after box of hamburger patties. His sister also worked there, and she got mad and quit. Bonus! Two down and how many to go?

CHAPTER 20

New Baby

When I started working at the fast-food place, my wife was about seven months pregnant. Things were going well, and the prognosis was good. We didn't have ultrasound back then, so we had no idea of the sex of the baby and really didn't care. We just wanted healthy. The baby was due on the tenth of April, and my wife went for her final checkup sometime around the last week of March. She went to the same country doctor as before. He checked her over and told her to go to the store and get a bottle of castor oil. She was to go home, drink half of it, wait a couple of hours, and drink the rest. He said everything looked fine, and he believed that with the castor oil, we would have a baby in the next few days. Like fools, we did what he said. She went home and drank the medicine as the doctor ordered, waited a few hours, and then drank the other half of the castor oil.

I went to work as normal. On April 4 I was scheduled to close the restaurant. About 1:30 in the morning, as I was counting the day's receipts, the store phone rang. I answered it only to hear my wife screaming on the other end. She didn't say anything, just screamed. I knew immediately that something was badly wrong and panicked. We had made all sorts of contingency plans, but they were for the tenth not the fourth. So I ran out of the store, leaving the back door open and over $2,000 on the table. I jumped in our old car and tore out for the house. When I got home, she was on her knees on the floor, leaning across the couch and squalling.

It was clear that the baby was coming and coming fast. We threw the suitcase we packed into the car and started for the hospital. I had to put her in the backseat, with her knees on the floor and leaning over the seat. That was the only reasonably comfortable way she could ride. We lived about six miles from town, out on the Dalton highway, and at 2:00 a.m., there was not a lot of traffic. We had gone two or three miles when the car sputtered to a stop, and I coasted to the side of the road. We were out of gas!

There was a gas station on the same lot as the restaurant, and I drove right past it on my way home. In my state of mind at the time, it never dawned on me to check the gas gauge and fill up before going home. Well it was too late now to worry about that. I had to find a phone and get an ambulance quickly. I left her in the backseat and ran down the road. There were very few houses along the road, and no one was awake.

I ran up to the first house I came to and banged on the door. After a couple of minutes, an elderly woman came to the door and peeked out behind the curtain on the door window. "Get off my porch," she yelled. I told her who I was and that I needed to use the phone quickly. I explained that my wife was down the highway and was going to have a baby all alone in the backseat if I didn't get her an ambulance. She yelled for me to leave again and said that she was going to call the sheriff if I didn't. I couldn't wait anymore, so I left her porch. But before I did, I yelled that if anything happened to my baby, I was going to come back and burn her house down with her inside.

I ran down the road for what seemed like miles and miles. Suddenly, I heard music in the distance. I couldn't believe my ears; there was actually somebody awake somewhere. I ran toward the source of the music and came to a big, old, house just off the highway. Several people were in the yard, dancing to the music. These people were genuine hippie flower children. The women were dressed in long, flowing dresses, and they moved around like they were in a trance. Several men loitered around, with the same blank look on their faces. I ran up to one of the men, and he immediately knew something was wrong. I told him that I needed to use a phone. He said, "Like wow, man. We don't like have a phone, man." He was clearly stoned but seemed to comprehend, so I told him that my wife was down the highway, having a baby in the car, and I needed to get her to the hospital. He said that they didn't have a phone but had an old car that ran. The problem was it didn't have any mufflers or plates, and he didn't have a driver's license. I told him that if he got stopped, I would take care of it.

We jumped into the worst relic that I have ever ridden in. It was an old Buick that not only did not have any mufflers, it didn't have half its floorboards. It was rusty and rattled like crazy, but it ran. The driver and another man were in the front, and I sat in the back. We tore down the highway like we had just robbed a bank, blowing through red lights and stop signs. We finally made it to my car. As we pulled up, I could see my wife's hand sticking out of the window, faintly trying to wave us down. I jumped out of the car, ran over to her, and helped her up. We managed to get her to the old Buick and onto the back floorboard. She was crying and yelling like crazy, and I had no idea how much time we had. For all I knew, she could have been already having the baby in the backseat.

The hippies jumped into the old car and gunned it for the hospital. They really began to get into it. They became emergency vehicle drivers, with the passenger checking for traffic and giving instructions to the driver. When they came to a red light, the passenger yelled out, "It's clear, man, go, go!" We finally made it to the emergency room of Bradley Memorial Hospital, and the driver slid to a stop.

I ran in and got an orderly to take a wheelchair out to her and get her into the hospital. The receptionist handed me a bunch of papers to sign, while my wife was sitting there, waiting. I told the receptionist my wife needed to see a doctor quick, but she insisted that I fill out all the papers. About that time my wife screamed, and the receptionist finally realized this was serious. She yelled at the orderly to get my wife upstairs and told me that I could fill out the papers later.

I took the elevator to the maternity ward. As I started to sit down, a nurse came in and said I could see the baby now. My son was born nine minutes after we checked in. My wife was basically having him as she was wheeled to the ward. Of course, there was no time for any prep or anything. She still had all her jewelry on and was in the same clothes. She had her front partial in at that time and refused to let the nurse take it out. The traumatic birth she went through left her pretty badly torn, and she had to stay in the hospital a couple of extra days.

Lots of people think we named our son Bradley after the name of the hospital. But the truth is we named him after a star from a soap opera my wife watched.

When we could finally take the baby home, we drove by the house where the hippies lived. There they were, still out in the yard, dancing around just like the night the baby came. I took the baby out of the car and over to them. I let several of them hold him and pass him around. They thought it was so cool they were involved in the birth of a baby. The thing I regret the most out of this story is that I never got any of their names. I would love to see any of them today and tell them how much I appreciate what they did that night. I did go back some time later, but they were gone. Sadly, I will never know where they went or who they were, but I will always be grateful to them.

CHAPTER 21

Police Officer

While we were in the hospital, my mother came to see the baby. All her anguish, hatred, stubbornness, and mean spirit immediately went away the first time she laid eyes on her beautiful, healthy grandson. She bonded with him instantly, and from that moment until she passed away, they were as close as two people could be. She literally worshipped him, and he felt the same way about her. All of a sudden the girl she couldn't stand was the apple of her eye, and she started lavishing attention on my wife as if nothing had ever happened between them. Brad was a great baby and was really no trouble at all, other than some ear-related problems. He was fun to be with, and having him completed the family circle we had looked for all those years.

About a couple of months after my son was born, the owner of the restaurant approached me about buying a house. A friend of his was a big-time, real-estate salesman in town and had found out about a new government program designed to encourage home ownership. I could buy a new house with no money down, and because of the program, the payments were low enough for me to make. I applied for the program and was approved. When Brad was about six months old, we moved into a brand-new house. I was twenty-three years old and a homeowner. *Pretty good for a high school dropout from Alabama,* I thought. The house was a really nice one out in the country. I managed to buy the empty lot next door from the builder, and that made a nice big yard for the baby.

I continued to manage the restaurant, and on weekends, several couples went dancing with us at the American Legion. The place had a great dance floor and always had a local band playing. One night one of the women who went with us decided it would be fun to play a trick on me. She told the guys in the band that I was a famous singer from Florida. If they asked me real nice, I would probably do a song for the crowd, which would be a real treat, seeing as how I was famous and all. The band fell for it and told the crowd just what she had told them. "A real famous singer from Florida is here, and we are gonna get him up here right now to sing one for you. Give a big round of applause for David from Florida."

Now I wasn't in on the joke and certainly didn't have a song prepared, nor was I sure that I could even sing. Nevertheless, the beer convinced me that I could do this, so I got up and went to the stage. The lead singer for the band asked me what I wanted to do, and the only thing I could think of was "Almost Persuaded," a song that was a big hit on the country charts at the time and pretty easy to sing. I knew the words. They asked me what key I wanted, and I said "Ah, don't worry about a key, I'll just start, and you come in however you want to." So I started the song off, and the band jumped in. It didn't sound too bad, actually. I finished the song, thanked the band, and went to sit down. The woman was cracking up at the joke, but it really turned out to be on her because the crowd acted like they loved it. At any rate, that was my debut as a singer.

Sometime later, one of my employees started talking about playing in a band once. He was a strange character, who normally worked on merchant ships as a crew member. He had taken some time off from being at sea and took a job with me in the meantime. We got to talking about what it would take to start a band. He played drums, and I happened to have a professional set of Ludwig drums that I had bought and was trying to learn to play. I also had an amplifier, mikes, and a guitar. (Remember the Gibson?) He knew a woman who could play piano and organ, so all we needed was a bass and lead guitar, and we would be in business. We found both, and they were interested. These two guys had been on a USO tour and were taking some time off from traveling, so a little hometown band was just the ticket. All we had to do was find an organ, and we were ready for gigs. I went down to a local music dealer who sold Hammond organs and convinced him that we were the real deal and going to be big. In exchange for lending us an organ, we would advertise his store every time we played. Believe it or not, he loaned us a brand-new Hammond B3 organ with a Leslie speaker. At the time, this thing probably cost over $10,000. All we had to do now was find a gig and start playing.

Notice I didn't say anything about practicing or rehearsal, just a gig to play. We found one pretty quickly, playing at the VFW on Friday and Saturday nights. I think we got paid $100 for each night, which came to about $20 apiece. We weren't doing it for money anyway, so that didn't matter. The woman who played the organ was one of the most talented musicians I have ever known. She could play anything in any genre. She could play by ear or read music. All the rest of us had to do was keep up and be in a close enough key. The drummer was pretty good, and the two guitar players were excellent and experienced. I became the lead singer and announcer. The problem was I didn't know ten songs, if that many. So we had to do a lot of ad-libbing and learning on the run. We bought "fake books" and started building our song base as we went.

We probably played there six months or more. One night we played for a private party for some big shots from the TVA. After several drinks I guess we started sounding pretty good because one of the senior guys came over during a break and offered us a job traveling around and doing these parties. It would have been a steady gig, and it didn't pay all that bad, but it meant all of us would have to quit our jobs and go on the road. We talked it over and came to the only logical conclusion, which was that we had to pass. I have often wondered what life would have been like if we had taken the gig. Who knows? We might have been famous. Sadly, after about six months, we broke up the band and went our separate ways. I enjoyed the experience and can always say that I played in a band, even if it was just thrown together. And when someone makes a snide comment about my singing, I can say, "I bet that I have made more money singing than you have as a music critic." That usually shuts them up.

Even though my wife and I both worked full time, it seemed like we could never get ahead. I am sure the biggest problem was our lack of money management. But no matter, we were always broke. Most of the time we drove an old clunker car and wondered every morning if it was going to start.

One memory that stands out in particular was when we were invited to go to Atlanta with another couple. We knew that we didn't have any money when we left but decided to go anyway. On the way down, they decided to stop to eat at a diner in Cartersville. We went in with them, even though we couldn't afford to eat. I think we had maybe a dollar between us. So we made up some excuse why we weren't hungry. We didn't want our child to be hungry, so we ordered a serving of mashed potatoes for him to eat. We were way too proud to let the other couple buy our supper, and as long as Bradley ate, we were good to go. We survived the trip with our pride intact and returned home to review our circumstances.

Around this time I started hanging out with several police officers from the local force, who came by the restaurant where I worked. I was in awe of their "war stories" and wild tales of adventure. I had never considered being a police officer and had spent most of my life far on the other side. These guys talked me into coming along for a ride a couple of times, and I was hooked. I decided right then that I wanted to be a police officer. The only problem was that at the time, you had to know somebody to get hired. I didn't know anyone except these guys. But as I had with many other things, once I made up my mind about being an officer, I was determined to make it work. I found out about a police reserve program with the department and immediately signed up. Just like that, I was a police officer. There was no requirement back then to go to a police academy, so I just put on a uniform and badge, and that was it. I started working as many nights as I could and still keep my job. I worked ball games, parades, festivals, or anything that got me out on the street. I started thinking about college again and looked into what programs were available at the junior college. I found out that there was a law enforcement degree that sounded just like what I wanted.

About this time, I was becoming very unhappy at the restaurant. I had worked extremely hard for the owner only to be forced to hire his brother-in-law as a submanager. He was going to college himself and wanted special hours to facilitate his schedule. I put up with this until one day I happened to see his check. Payroll was the only aspect of managing the restaurant that was done by someone else, so I had no idea what he made. His check was $50 a week more than I was making to manage the place. I was livid! I went to the owner and confronted him about it. I demanded to be paid at least the same, or I was walking. He really insulted me by offering me a $5 per week raise, so I quit right then and there. I had put my life on hold for him and made extreme sacrifices for the store. This was the thanks that I got? I was outa there.

I left the restaurant and once again found myself unemployed. So I really started pushing to get into college. I worked every opportunity I had at the police department but had to find something that paid money and fast. Over the next few months, I sold insurance, drove a truck, and owned a restaurant. The restaurant was actually a big snack bar located in a bowling alley. A group of investors bought the restaurant equipment and leased it to me to run. Once again, I took money from my wife's salary to put into the cash register. I hung onto this adventure about six months or so, but just couldn't get it to work. I managed to get most of my money out and closed another chapter of my life. I decided to get out of the restaurant business for good. By now I had worked for seven different chains, owned a snack bar in a pharmacy, and owned this one. All had taken years off my life and left me with nothing. It was time to find a new way of making a living.

I was finally accepted in the law enforcement degree program at Cleveland State Community College. I was accepted around October, but classes would not start until January. So I had to find work until then.

Cleveland is known as the headquarters of several major churches. The Church of God, Church of God of Prophecy, and the Church of God of Jerusalem Acres, among others, call Cleveland home. The Church of God of Prophecy decided to build a brand-new world headquarters building in Cleveland and was hiring workers just as I needed a job. I applied and went to work almost immediately. It was winter, and it gets very cold in Cleveland. Nevertheless, I hung in there until January, and as soon as classes started, quit my one and only construction job.

The law enforcement degree program was run by a neat old guy named Stubbs. Mr. Stubbs was retired from the US Air Force, where he was a lawyer assigned to the Judge Advocate General Corps. He was a smart guy but knew absolutely nothing about police work and most of the time just stumbled along. He was good to the students, however, and especially liked me for some reason. He helped me get started and acted as my guidance counselor at first. Most of the embedded axioms of law that I call on every day I learned from him. I can still hear him reciting case law, so evidently he made an impression on me.

Going back to school required a totally different way of thinking. It had been many years since I had been in a classroom, and I wasn't the best of students then. I had to keep telling myself that I was in "big school" now. No more goofing off. I had to knuckle down and actually study. Going from the tenth grade in high school to college is quite a jump. I was behind almost immediately and on a fast-moving train that wouldn't wait. I was studying college-level biology having never taken high school biology. The one thing in my favor was that I could read at a high level.

I had earned the GI bill from my years in the navy, and now was the time to use it. That benefit is probably one of the most important that a servicemember can earn. I received a monthly check, which more than paid for tuition and books. There was actually some left over for living expenses. We were still struggling financially, though, so I had to find work fast. I was still getting a lot of hours with the police department, but it wasn't enough. I needed a job that allowed me to go to school during the day, so I applied for a security guard job at a local plant. It was easy work and fit right in with my school schedule. The job was at a huge vinyl plastics plant that made fabric for furniture.

I worked third shift, and when I got off, I went straight to school. I usually had class until about two or three o'clock. Then I slept for a couple hours before starting all over again.

There was only one other person in the plant after midnight. Johnny ran the boiler system and was without doubt the wildest person I have ever met. He also became my best friend. Our relationship started out as two guys trying to pass the time until daylight and trying to stay awake. Johnny was redneck personified. Everything about him said, "Don't mess with me, or I will blow your house apart." He was a small man, maybe 5'7" or 8", with a slender but muscular build. He smoked and drank heavily and, I suspect, wasn't above doing a lot more. At the time he was married to the sweetest woman on earth. He invited me over to their house a couple of times early on to play cards, and she was the consummate host.

At first we were just coworkers, trying to get by. But then the great flood happened. My wife and I sold the house we had bought and moved into a duplex apartment just after I started to school. It started raining one day and rained for almost a week straight. I worked my regular shift at the plant, went to class, and came home for some sleep. It was still raining hard when I went to bed, but I didn't think anything of it, until a couple of hours later, our phone rang. It was a neighbor calling to tell us to get out of the house because the water was rising. I stumbled out of bed and looked out in our yard to see water already pouring over the steps and into the apartment. I grabbed as much as I could and moved it to higher ground inside the house, but there was not much that I could do. I got into my truck and headed to the plant where my wife worked and to the day care to pick up my son.

When I left, there was maybe a foot of water in the yard, and it was maybe up to the wheels on our old car, which was still in the driveway. It had a flat that morning, so I had taken my wife to work before going to class. I was gone maybe an hour, and when we got home, the car was completely underwater, and water was up over the porch. I waded to the door, and when I looked inside, I almost passed out. Everything we owned was underwater. Later, when the water finally subsided, we measured the silt line on the walls. There had been over four feet of water inside the house.

Now we were essentially homeless. I had no idea who to call or where to go, so I called Johnny. Without hesitation, he told us to come to his house. He moved his three kids around and made room for us to live with them until we could find another place. At the time, we had no idea what was going to happen. All we knew was that everything we owned was gone.

Fortunately, the president declared east Tennessee a federal disaster area, and that meant we would get some money for assistance. I have to give kudos to the government and to several service organizations as well. They really stepped up. We received a forgivable loan for over $5,000, food stamps, and a stipend to buy cleaning supplies. The Red Cross stepped up with clothing for all of us, as well as bedding and some money.

We lived with Johnny for three weeks. That's three extra people in a house that was already crowded with his family. But neither Johnny nor his wife, Faye, ever complained in any way. They never asked for a penny; it was all heart. I became indebted to Johnny that day, even though he never looked at it that way. He was just helping out a friend.

I had a lot of adventures with him over the years, and we never had a cross word—even though Johnny could be the most aggravating person you ever met when he was drinking. He never challenged me, and I always had his back. I saw Johnny do some crazy things in the years that I knew him, some that would put most men in jail. He seemed to have a guardian angel that kept him out of real trouble.

For several years, even after I went to work full time on the police force, we went to the American Legion on Saturday and danced all night. There were usually ten or more of us. We sat at a long table, and everybody danced with whomever they liked. It was all innocent, and nobody went home with somebody else's wife or girlfriend. For the most part, Johnny was tolerant of outsiders asking Faye to dance, if the person was a gentleman about it and if she wanted to. One night we were there having a great time, and some guy came from across the floor and asked her to dance. The guy was three sheets in the wind already and could barely stand up long enough to get the words slurred out of his mouth. Faye politely declined his generous offer to dance, and he went away. The next song, he was back again. Same thing: she declined; he went away. Then he came back a third time, and that was it. Johnny said, "Mister, three times is enough," and came across the table, knocking him to the floor. Well, when a punch is thrown in a dancehall, that's all it takes to start a riot. People were swinging at people who had nothing to do with the fight. Women screamed, and someone called the police. I hustled my wife, Faye, and Johnny to the back door and out to our car. As we pulled out of the parking lot onto the highway, I could see blue lights racing to the hall.

Another time, Johnny was at a turkey shoot, where people shoot at targets with a shotgun, and the closest to an X wins a turkey or ham. Johnny had won several times when this guy got jealous and started accusing him of cheating. Now I don't know how you could cheat at a turkey shoot, but he kept insisting that Johnny did. Johnny told the guy to leave him alone, that he just wanted to shoot and have a good time, but the guy kept on. After a while, Johnny got his stuff and headed for his car, and the guy followed him. When Johnny got to his car, the guy reached out and put his hand on Johnny's shoulder, as if to spin him around. As soon as his hand touched him, Johnny came around with a hunting knife and plunged it into his stomach. Johnny reached down and pulled out his knife and left the guy there in the parking lot. The guy lived, and Johnny was never questioned about the incident. I still have the knife that he used.

The most dangerous thing that I ever experienced involving Johnny was on a motorcycle ride to the mountains of North Carolina. Back then you could buy cigarettes in North Carolina tax free at a really good price. You could legally purchase and have in your possession ten cartons. North Carolina was about forty or fifty miles from Cleveland, and it made for a nice ride on a pretty day. We would ride up, make a day of it, buy twenty cartons of cigarettes per couple, and ride back home. We would sell the cigarettes and make enough to pay for the trip. It was all completely legal, and we got in some real good rides that way. But on one ride, we got to North Carolina and stopped just across the line at a little store that sold gas, eight-track tapes, some groceries, and cigarettes. Johnny bought the usual twenty cartons for him and Faye and left the bag on the counter while they looked over the tape selection just a couple of feet away. When they were finished, Johnny went to retrieve the bag of cigarettes, but they were gone. Johnny demanded of the counterperson what happened to his cigarettes, and the guy said, "Man, I am sorry. That guy there picked them up, and I thought they were his."

Johnny went tearing out of the building, yelling, "Let's go!" When we got outside it was pouring down rain, but Johnny fired up his 750 Honda, and Faye jumped on the back. My wife and I made it to our bike and took off after them. It was raining so hard that we could barely see. With an inch or more of water on the road it could not have been more dangerous, but I knew that if Johnny caught this person and I wasn't close by, he would kill him before I could get there. My wife was barely hanging on and was soaking wet as we tore down the road at over eighty miles an hour. That is dangerous on dry pavement. It is insane in weather like that! I could barely see Johnny's taillights ahead. As we topped a rise in the road, I saw Johnny's bike on the side of the road, with a car pulled over next to the barrier. Johnny had dragged the guy out of the car and had him over the trunk, beating the daylights out of him. I slid to a stop and yelled at the top of my lungs for him to let him go. I managed to get Johnny off him long enough for him to say that it was a mistake, that he had gotten the wrong bag at the counter. We brushed the guy off, put him back in his car, took the bag of cigarettes, and headed home. Just another "Johnny" day.

I suppose I could be criticized for condoning Johnny's activities and not taking legal steps, since I was now on the way to becoming a police officer. I will leave that discussion with this thought. Johnny was the best friend I have ever had. He was loyal when fair-weather friends left my wife or me. And he never wavered in his friendship. He never asked me to do anything illegal, nor did he ever expect me to do anything for him or anyone else. Johnny was actually a good person who only wanted to be left alone, but if he didn't get what he wanted, someone was going to pay.

I continued to work as a security guard and go to school full time until about the midway point of the first semester. I heard through the grapevine that there was an opening for a full-time officer on the police department, and I submitted an application. As I mentioned earlier, the only way that you could get on the force was to know someone with influence, and I didn't know anyone who fit the bill. I applied anyway and was shocked to learn that I was going to be interviewed. I went in on the appointed day and sat down with the chief, who asked me some general questions and made a few general statements regarding the job. This particular chief had been there since the beginning of time and knew everybody, and everybody knew him. He was an "old school" chief who knew how to play the political game very well.

At the time, each member of the city council was responsible for an element of city services. The most sought after position was that of police commissioner. The position really didn't have any authority, but the name made it the most valuable one on council. Most council members lucky enough to draw this assignment carried a badge of their office, and some even had radios assigned to them, so they could monitor police traffic. At the time of my application, the police commissioner was a personnel officer for a local car dealership. The chief told me at the conclusion of my interview that he had no problem hiring me, but the commissioner would have the final say. So I made an appointment with him.

On the day of the appointment, he asked me several questions about myself and what I wanted to do. I answered all his questions, and at some point during the interview, I figured that I should lay all my cards on the table about what I would and would not do. It was widely rumored that police officers were expected to campaign for those elected officials responsible for their jobs. City vehicles were routinely used to transport voters or to carry signs to a potential supporter's house. Of course, you were supposed to know who certain supporters were and never ticket those valuable folks. That didn't set well with me, even back then. I had made up my mind long before the interview that I wasn't going to be that kind of officer. I told the commissioner right there in his office that if he hired me, I would not campaign for him. I also told him that I certainly wouldn't campaign against him; I wasn't going to get involved in politics period. The moment I said it I figured the interview was over and that he was going to throw me out of his office. To my surprise, he said that he didn't expect officers to do that and actually frowned on those who did. He told me that he was impressed with me and would recommend to the chief that I be hired. Just like that I was a full-time police officer, the last person on the face of the earth anyone would have expected to have such a job.

In those days, even full-time regular officers rarely went to the academy for training. There was only one academy for the entire state and going was not a requirement. There was also no field training like there is today. You were basically on your own to learn as you went. I had asked to be placed on the third shift so I could attend class during the day. The chief was gracious enough to accommodate that request, and on the appointed night, I reported for duty at 11:00 p.m. The shift sergeant gave some briefing points and then told me to get the keys to a certain patrol unit. He told me to "Just stay on the south side, and if you need me, call." I went out into the parking lot, found the assigned vehicle, fired it up, and was on my way. Police Officer Dave was on duty! I had ridden with several officers as a reservist, so I was not completely clueless, but I had never ridden a call by myself.

I just pulled out of the parking lot when I got my first call as a police officer. The call was to a local drive-in that was a popular after-hours hangout and attracted a lot of drive-around traffic. A nice old guy lived in a trailer adjacent to the restaurant property, and he had a big German shepherd. Normally the dog was as tame as could be, but on this night, a group of motorcyclists were riding around and around the property, whooping and hollering and generally causing a ruckus. The dog took it as long as it could, but after a while, the dog had enough. When one of the bikers kicked at it as they rode by, the dog grabbed the guy and dragged him off the bike. The biker and his ride went head over teakettle, resulting in road rash and some scratches on the bike. The biker jumped up and was going to hurt the dog, until the owner ran up with a shotgun. So now we had a "Mexican standoff," and someone called the police.

"Officer Dave here. What seems to be the problem?" The biker was yelling and cursing, demanding that I have the dog put to sleep.

The owner was still threatening to shoot the biker. The biker wanted the owner to pay for the damage to his bike, and so on, and so on. Unfortunately, everyone had been drinking. Today I would have arrested the biker for DUI, but back then it was more common. I just told everyone to go their separate ways, or I was going to arrest them all. That seemed to get their attention and resulted in a peaceful outcome.

Later on, the department started riding two to a car, and I had a partner on most shifts. The very first officer that I was assigned with was an old guy who had been on the department forever. He knew that I was going to college, and on the first night we were together, he let me know who was boss in the car. As soon as we left the parking lot, he said to me, "Don't try to tell me nothing, college boy. I got twenty years of experience." I soon learned what his experience consisted of, and it had nothing to do with being an effective police officer. He knew every place in town that gave free meals to police officers, every good place to hide and sleep, and a thousand ways to get out of answering a call. As a result of his partnership, I realized early in my career that there was twenty years of experience and there was one year of experience times twenty.

I was determined that staying in school was my first and foremost priority, and everything else would just have to work around it. I was working full time as a police officer and taking a full load in college. There were many days that I functioned on two hours of sleep, and I usually took an alarm clock to school with me just in case I had a few minutes to nap between classes. Of course at this same time, I had an infant at home who had the usual childhood medical problems that often required that my wife or I be up with him. There were many nights that I walked the hall, holding him and sleeping at the same time.

I actually got pretty good at it. My wife and I took turns so that both of us got as much sleep as possible. On the nights that I rode alone, it was pretty bad, especially just before daybreak. One night I was awakened by someone blowing a horn behind me. When I sat up, I was at a traffic light, in the middle of the street. I had stopped for the light and gone straight to sleep. I have no idea how long I had been there before the other car came along, but that night certainly got my attention.

Another very important event that occurred about the same time I started college was I quit smoking. I started school in January and had made quitting my New Year's resolution. I went on patrol December 28 on my regular third shift with a full pack of cigarettes. I had been on the job about an hour and just out of the blue decided that was the night. I pulled up to a trash can, threw a whole pack into it, and drove away. That was a long time ago, and I haven't smoked since. I went from three packs a day to zero in one night, and I did it cold turkey. No patches, no gum, nothing but determination. I had this attitude that I was making a turn in my life, and if I were ever going to accomplish anything, I had to quit smoking first. If I couldn't do that, nothing else would be possible. Quitting was undoubtedly the hardest single thing that I have ever done. Today I measure difficulty by that standard, and it has helped me get through some tough situations. When I quit, cigarettes were fifty cents a pack and had just gone up to that amount days before I quit. One thing is for sure: I didn't quit for money, but it did help. I have saved thousands of dollars over the years and have probably paid for a very nice car with the money I didn't spend on smokes. There have been other positive aspects of quitting as well, such as health issues. I certainly would not have made it in my career choice had I not quit and gotten into some semblance of good physical condition.

So at this time I had a new job with lots of stress, I was going to college full time, and I had quit smoking. If I could handle all of this, nothing else could bother me.

Things were going great, until one day the chief called me into his office and informed me that I was being reassigned to day shift. This was a crushing blow because I was right in the middle of classes. I didn't have any other choice except to go along with it if I wanted to continue with the department. I made arrangements to take night classes and even talked the chief into allowing me to take some classes on duty occasionally. It was more difficult, and day shift was nothing like nights. In fact, it was boring.

I was really at a turning point in my job, when one day a decision was clearly handed to me in the form of an accident. I was on patrol on the south end of town one afternoon, and it was freezing cold out. I drove across a big cemetery that was high up on a hill, and as I started down the other side, I hit a patch of ice in the road and began to skid down the hill sideways. As luck would have it, a pickup was coming up the hill toward me, and we got to a curve at the same time. My vehicle was totally out of control, and I slid into the side of the truck. The vehicle that I was assigned to was a pool car and not in very good mechanical condition. For one thing, it had almost no tire tread and bad brakes, so there was no avoiding the accident other than not driving on that roadway.

I called in and reported the accident, which triggered the on-duty lieutenant coming to the scene. He was an old-school police officer, much like my first partner. When he got there, he surveyed the situation and informed me that I was being suspended for two weeks. That is two weeks without pay for an accident that could not be avoided and that had a damage of maybe two hundred dollars at most. I told him that I didn't think that was fair, but he held his ground and blamed the chief for the decision. The suspension was the final straw that determined my decision to leave the department.

A good friend of mine, who was a detective when I first joined the department, had run for sheriff and won. When he was running, he told me that if he won, he wanted me to work for him. Now was the time to put his word to the test. I parked the patrol car back at the station and drove my personal car over to the sheriff's office. I told him what happened, and he told me I could go to work the next day if I wanted. I called the police department and quit on the spot. So now I was a deputy sheriff! The sheriff allowed me to pick my shift, which, of course, was nights.

CHAPTER 22

Deputy Dave

Joining the sheriff's department was an experience unlike any other. The new sheriff had taken over a department that was completely shot out. Patrol cars were junk. There was little or no equipment, and all new personnel. Most Southern sheriffs fire everyone as soon as they take office and fill those positions with handpicked staff. This is understood when you become a deputy, and this sheriff was no different. I could question some of his hiring decisions, but at the time, I really didn't care. I just wanted to work. To say this bunch were all misfits would be an understatement. Even the senior staff had questionable backgrounds, and some of the deputies were more than questionable. I have to say the short time that I was with the sheriff was probably the most fun of any job I have ever had.

It was a wild ride to say the least. I worked the night shift, from 11:00 p.m. until 7:00 a.m., six days a week. If I had court, that was on my own time. You had to be in court, and you didn't get paid or get time off. You just sucked it up and complied. That was the cost of being a deputy.

Working at the sheriff's department was, in many respects, exactly like the police department. One particular similarity was that you had to buy your own equipment. When I went to work for the police department, I had to buy my own gun, gun belt, uniforms, badge, and other equipment I might need on the job. Working for the sheriff was the same. Fortunately, a lot of the equipment that I had bought while working at the police department would work in my new job.

An interesting aspect of working in law enforcement back then was that you could carry any weapon you chose. It was your money, so you could carry whatever you fancied. Some guys went all out and bought the biggest gun they could find. Some carried carbine rifles as backup weapons. Many nights, I went on patrol with a 30-30 Winchester rifle sitting on the seat beside me. I looked like John Wayne when I got out of the car.

On most nights there were only two deputies on duty for the entire county, which meant you were on your own out there. If a bad fight broke out or some other violent crime took place, you really had to be on your guard because help probably wasn't coming anytime soon.

Right after I joined the department, one of the deputies seized a large amount of marijuana from a traffic stop over on the interstate. The deputy had been following a suspicious car when the driver got scared and started to run. As he pulled away from the deputy, he threw a large garbage bag out the window. The deputy stopped, grabbed the bag, and continued on after the suspect, catching him a short time later. He took the bag of dope back to the sheriff's office, turned it over to the detective division, and finished out his shift.

When I came on at 11:00 p.m., there was extra staff working; we were planning on doing a warrant sweep that night. We met in the detective office to get our plan together and decide exactly where we were going. The big bag of dope was still sitting there on the desk, and all the deputies were admiring the find. One of the deputies was the lead detective, and one was the shift supervisor. There were about six people in the room, including another deputy, also named David. David was about the same age as I, with about as much experience. He was a great guy, and tonight would test his integrity as a deputy like no other night.

While we were standing around, one of the deputies made a comment about the dope, saying that he bet that it was some "good stuff." That led to someone else suggesting that we try it, which led to someone rolling a joint. So right there in the detective office of the sheriff's department were a bunch of deputies smoking dope. They passed the joint around to everybody in the room. When it got to me and David, we declined. Both of us knew that what they were doing was wrong, but the "code" kept us from arresting everyone on the spot. We just knew that we were not going to be a part of the party.

They finished the joint and may have rolled another. I don't remember for sure. When the dope smoking was done, we loaded up in one patrol vehicle and took off to serve the warrants. The most important part of what I just said was that we were all in the same car, so none of us could have called anyone while we were gone. We had gone maybe ten miles when the sheriff came on the radio and told us to come back to the department, ASAP. We turned around immediately and drove back to the station.

When we got there, the sheriff, the chief of police, and the district attorney were waiting on us. The sheriff called each of us into his office, read us the Miranda warning, and questioned us about the dope smoking. Fortunately, I went in first. When he asked me who was smoking dope in the detective office, I responded that I would not tell him who was smoking, but David and I were not. I told him he would have to find out any other information on his own.

He thanked me for being honest with him and said that he was glad to hear I wasn't a part of the incident. He excused me and told me to return to patrol, along with David. We spent the rest of the night trying to figure out how the sheriff knew about the incident so quickly. To this day, I do not know the answer. We were both relieved we were all in the car because had we not been, we would have been singled out as snitches for sure.

I finished the shift and went to class. When class was over I went home. I had just gone to bed when my phone rang. It was the sheriff, asking me why I wasn't at work. I told him that my shift was from 11:00 p.m. until 7:00 a.m., and I was trying to get some sleep. He said detectives work from 7:00 p.m. until 7:00 a.m. I told him I was not a detective. He said, "You are now. Get to work." He had fired the detective who was involved and was replacing him with me. Now the only problem with this picture was that I knew nothing about investigations. I had never even been to a crime scene at that time. But I dragged myself up, got dressed, and went into work. I was assigned one of the detective vehicles. When I went out to get in, I checked the trunk and noticed all sorts of boxes of equipment inside. There were print kits, cameras, and plaster of paris kits. These were all the tools you would need to be a crime fighter.

The sheriff was waiting on me when I got to the station and called me into his office. We never discussed the dope incident again. We just got down to business. He told me that there had been a break-in at the home of a dairy farmer way out in the country, and these folks were big contributors to his campaign. That translated into "special attention needed," so I loaded up and drove out there.

I found the house and went inside to survey the break-in. The house was a big, old, two-story house. The perpetrator had climbed the outside stair case up to the second floor, broke out a glass in the door, and went in. He had stolen several items of jewelry and some musical instruments, including a rare mandolin. I walked around, trying to act like I knew what I was doing. I had taken the camera up with me and was taking some crime scene pictures when the farmer asked me if I was going to take fingerprints. "Of course I am going to dust for prints. I was just getting ready to do that," I replied confidently. I went out to the patrol car and opened the trunk. I really didn't know what I was looking for, but when I saw that one of the boxes said print kit, I figured that was just what I needed.

I took the box up to the bedroom and told the farmer that I needed to be in the room alone while I dusted. He didn't question me and left me in there by myself. I closed the bedroom door and sat on the floor with the box. Fortunately for me, there was an instruction booklet inside the box, and I sat there on his bedroom floor and taught myself how to lift prints. I threw print dust all over that room and actually lifted some pretty good prints. The farmer never knew that I didn't have a clue about what I was doing. He probably thought I was an experienced investigator by the way I acted. After all, I was specially chosen for that particular crime.

When I had sufficiently fooled the farmer, I packed up my kits and drove back to the station to report to the sheriff. I figured that the key to solving the crime was going to be the mandolin because the rest of the stuff would be hard to identify.

A couple of days after the break-in, I happened to visit one of the local pawnshops. I don't remember exactly why I was there. It could have been personal business. Nevertheless, I was in there, looking around. On the wall with the other instruments was a Gibson mandolin, matching the description the farmer had given me. It was easy to identify because it had a tiny crack right at the sound opening on one side. I asked the shop owner where he had gotten it, and he said he bought it from some kids earlier in the day. I called the farmer, and he came down to the shop immediately and identified the mandolin as his. He was ecstatic. He just couldn't believe that I had found his heirloom instrument. Now all I had to do was find out who committed the crime.

The shop owner provided the best identification he could, which wasn't much. He did give me a pretty good vehicle description, and other than that, said it was just two young kids, one male and one female. I tracked down the vehicle based on the description he gave me and actually found the couple. I thought, *Man, I am closing in. I am about to make the arrest of my career.*

I brought the kids in for an interview only to find out they found the instrument on the side of the road and thought they could get some quick cash for it. A likely story for sure! I followed up on the story, including going to the area where they said the mandolin was found. I parked the car and walked up and down the roadway they had described. There in the tall grass beside the road was the case the instrument was in when taken from the farmhouse.

Whoever took it must have thought it wasn't worth anything and threw it out of the car. When it landed, the case came open, spilling the mandolin onto the roadway for the kids to find. I didn't arrest anyone on the case, but I did recover the most valuable item that had been stolen. The farmer called the sheriff and praised me big time for recovering his beloved instrument. He never knew that it was all pure luck and no skill. But in this business, I would rather be lucky than good any day.

There are so many crazy stories from the time I was at the sheriff's department. It's hard to decide which ones are worth talking about. One adventure that comes to mind sort of sums up the department. Several of us were working one night, shortly after I was promoted to detective, and it was slow and boring. Instead of going out looking for criminals, or doing some proactive patrolling, we decided it would be great fun to stage a pursuit with another vehicle.

There were two patrol cars sitting in a parking lot, with two deputies in each car. There were two other cars on the road in various parts of the county. We got on the radio and faked a vehicle stop for some minor infraction, and then frantically told the dispatcher the car was running on us. We took turns on the radio, giving direction of travel, speed, and other pertinent information. Police officers were coming from all over the place to get in on the chase. There were even officers spotting the alleged car that we were chasing.

This charade went on for almost an hour, until we decided that it was time to call it off. We came on the radio and told dispatch that he had turned off on a major highway and was almost to the county line. We called the chase off and supposedly went back to patrolling. No one ever knew that we had never left the parking lot.

On other slow nights we would all go rabbit hunting out in the country. The way that worked was two or three of us would get into one car, with one deputy sitting on the hood with a shotgun. We drove along some piece of desolate back road until we spotted a rabbit or coon from the roadway, and the person on the hood would open up with the shotgun. Really great police work, don't you think?

There were seven schools within the county, spread all over the place. We patrolled using the schools as landmarks and reference points. We were expected to circle each school at least once a shift, which was, at times, difficult to do. Once we arrived at one of the schools, we called dispatch and informed them we were at such and such school. Dispatch would log us in as having been to that part of the county. Some deputies spent the biggest part of a shift behind some church or in a cemetery, never going near one of the schools. They called in from their hiding places, and no one was the wiser.

The obvious problem in this whole picture was the lack of supervision. We were just a bunch of stupid kids, running around, doing whatever we could get away with. With any small amount of supervision, we would probably have made decent deputies. As it was, we were just out having fun.

One night we were standing in front of the sheriff's office, waiting to go on the road. A couple deputies decided to demonstrate their prowess with a pistol. One deputy would toss a coin in the air, and the other would draw his weapon and shoot at it. The sheriff's office was in the middle of town, and shots fired drew a lot of attention. Do you think that stopped them from doing something so crazy? No way! We were just a bunch of deputies having fun—nothing to worry about.

Not everything that went on at the department was all fun, and most of us knew where to draw the line between having a little fun and committing a criminal act. However, there were those deputies who didn't seem to know the difference. One night right after I started, I was assigned to ride with a particular deputy. We rode around awhile, getting acquainted. About midnight he drove to a house way out in the country. We drove around the house and pulled up in the back, next to a window. He got out and went over and tapped on the window. Some lady opened the window and slid a bag out to him. He went back to the trunk of our car, put the bag inside, and we went on our way.

He did this several other times, always following the same procedure. He would go up to the window—or in some cases a door—and come back with a bag. I had no idea what he was doing and didn't ask questions. When our shift was over, we came back to the station parking lot. He called me over and lifted the trunk lid. The trunk was full of grocery bags, and the bags were full of pints of whiskey. He said, "Here, take these," and handed me a couple of the bags. I asked him what they were, and he replied, "That's your cut." I asked, "Of what?" He replied, "For shaking down those bootleggers." What was happening, I learned, was that the houses that we went to sold illegal bootleg whiskey, and he knew about it. Once a week, he went around to all the houses and collected a "fee" for allowing them to operate. Well my momma didn't raise but one fool, and I wasn't about to get caught up in a scam like that, so I refused. I told him that whatever he was into was okay by me; I just wasn't going to get involved. He gladly took all the bags, and we never mentioned it again.

I heard a rumor that he later (after I left) shook down a truck driver with a load of furniture and got caught. I don't know if that was true, and I have no idea what happened to him.

One evening as I was out patrolling, I stopped a car for weaving and found the driver to be a very drunk woman. She had been drinking Bud all evening and was stoned. She could barely walk and had even more trouble talking. In addition to being almost dead-drunk, she had dipped snuff all evening and was a real mess. Snuff was running all down her front and all over the car. I put her in the back of my patrol car and headed for the department. Just as we got under way, she started flirting with me, telling me I was cute. She said that she would sleep with me if I just took her home. I kept driving, and she kept flirting.

I guess she realized it wasn't working and that I was going to take her to jail. So she asked me one more time to take her home. I didn't answer, and she asked, "You ain't gonna take me home?" I said, "No, I am not." Well she told me what I could do to myself and spit right through the screen, between the seats. It landed just below my hairline and ran down under the collar of my shirt. One cannot imagine grossness until some drunk spits snuff down his or her back. I had a sudden urge to give her a "screen test," but my better sense took over. I finally got her to a cell. It took every ounce of professionalism that I could muster to keep from hurting her bad.

I have never been shot in all the years I have spent in law enforcement. I have also never shot anyone. I have come awfully close on both counts. I have been shot at, but not close. One night I was sent to a domestic incident, which is probably the most dangerous situation that you can be in. When I got to the residence, it was obvious the husband had been drinking a lot and beaten his wife pretty badly.

This was before many of the domestic violence laws were enacted, and there wasn't much governing such situations. I decided to arrest the husband and charge him with assault due to the obvious injuries to the wife. I had barely gotten him into handcuffs when the wife ran to a closet and pulled out a shotgun. Fortunately for me, I was close to her when she came out with the gun and was able to grab it from her. I don't know if the gun was loaded, but I got it away from her and arrested her. She called for help, and when I tried to help her, she turned on me. Such is life!

The twelve-hour shifts started to have an effect on me, especially while going to school. When I first started college, I had made my mind up that nothing was going to interfere with my goal of finishing. But I was just barely getting by, and many days, I went to work with only two or fewer hours of sleep. There was no home life. And my son was suffering because the only time he saw me was when I was asleep. I started thinking hard about making a change. It just wasn't working. I asked the sheriff about putting me back on the road, but he wanted to keep me in the investigations office, so I reluctantly resigned.

Finishing school was just too important to me. By this time, there was a new chief at the police department, and he was a game changer. He had been the assistant chief and knew me. He offered to let me come back and work as much, or as little, as I needed. I remained with him until I finished college.

CHAPTER 23

The Road to Being a Gentleman

I settled into my new role as a part-time police officer and full-time student. I wound up working almost as many hours as before, but I could at least pick the schedule. School was progressing along, and graduation was on the horizon. I began to think about what to do after graduation. I knew for sure that I wanted to continue as a law enforcement officer in some capacity, and my degree was sure to prepare me for that. I took every law class I could find, as well as any other course that might further my career as a crime fighter. Back then, police officers were just about everything at a crime scene. Since we were almost always the first to arrive on a call, we were expected to deliver babies, splint fractures, stop the bleeding, and perform a long list of other emergency services, all while maintaining order and traffic flow. There were times when we had to grab a fire extinguisher and put out a fire or man a fire hose alongside a volunteer fireman. In short, we were jacks of all trades.

Since I wanted to be the best and know everything about my job, I became extremely interested in first aid and emergency medicine. I took every course that I could find and eventually took the emergency medical technician (EMT) course. I became a Red Cross first-aid instructor, as well as a CPR instructor. I lived and breathed emergency. I had red-light fever in the worst way, and I wanted to run every call, no matter what it was or how bad it was.

One thing that certainly changed in the previous year was that I was no longer picked on by anyone. I developed an extreme temper and didn't take anything off anyone. I didn't abuse anyone, but when I said "Move," I expected to see movement. I wasn't afraid of anyone or anything. In fact, I became invincible and bulletproof. When I went into the navy, I weighed 156 pounds, and when I came out, I still only weighed 165 pounds, soaking wet. Now 165 on a 6'3" frame doesn't make for much of a threat. When I would start to arrest someone I always got this look like. "Who you bringing with you 'cause you sure ain't gonna do it by yourself!" I needed to gain some weight fast. I set a goal of weighing 195 pounds and wanted to do it as soon as possible. I started a weight gain program that included drinking a protein milkshake several times a day. The shake was made up of a protein mix, milk, raw eggs, and blackstrap molasses. It tasted awful but seemed to work. And for the first time in my life, I started gaining weight. It wasn't long before the looks went away and people started listening to me when I told them to do something. That also meant fewer fights and less torn clothing.

Going to school full time and working full time didn't leave much time for any kind of recreation or relaxation. One of the few things that I enjoyed was hanging out with a buddy at a local coffee shop just before going to work. I also became a very good pinball player. Back when I ran the restaurant in a bowling alley, I met Adrian, who ran the alley. Adrian and I were about the same age and had served in the military. We became close friends. Later, we both entered college at the same time and actually took several classes together. His interests were different from mine, and he wanted to be an architect.

One of his few passions was playing pinball. He would hang out at this little coffee shop downtown and play pinball for hours. He introduced me to the game, and I started meeting him there before going to the police station for work. Now gambling was, of course, illegal in Tennessee at the time, and pinball paid out cash prizes. It was so rampant and such a part of the culture there that no one questioned it. Every truck stop, diner, café, and joint had several machines, and there was usually a waiting line to play. Pinball is a mechanical game that requires manual dexterity and luck to play, but the payoff can be substantial. Pinball was made famous by the movie *Tommy,* and the machines that we played on were exactly the same as in the movie.

Throughout my college career I was in a hurry. I wanted to complete whatever degree program I was in as soon as possible and move on. I think I invented the term "overload." Students could only take so many hours without permission from the dean. This was to prevent burnout and wasting the college's resources on failing students. I found a way around the system, however. I discovered early on that I could go into admissions during the drop/add period and add as many hours as I could stand. Somehow this didn't trigger any red flags, and it worked time and time again. I never took fewer than fifteen hours per semester and usually took more. The most that I took was twenty-one hours in one semester. Now that was burnout! I was on a mission, however, and survived.

Graduation day finally came, and I was approved to graduate. We were to graduate in the school's auditorium, and I invited my mother and Uncle Jack to the ceremony. I invited more of my relatives, but those two actually came. By now my son was about two and a half years old, three at the most. When I walked across the stage for my diploma he yelled out, "That's my daddy." The entire audience cracked up as he clapped his hands for me. What a feeling! I was actually a college graduate.

But now I was hungry and wanted more. I had previously started looking around trying to decide what I was going to do after graduation. I had looked at transferring to East Tennessee State or the University of Tennessee at Chattanooga (UTC) but had not completely made up my mind. East Tennessee had a criminal justice degree. UTC didn't, but it did have a similar program that would do in a pinch. Shortly after graduation my school held a career day on campus. Universities came from all over to pitch their wares and recruit students. I attended the program, hoping to get enough information to finally make my decision about where I was going to apply.

I was walking around, looking at the brochures on tables, when I happened to stop at one particular table. Behind the table were two guys dressed in funny uniforms with all sorts of ribbons and accoutrements. Something told me to inquire about their program, so I did. They explained that they were from the Reserve Officer Training Program at UTC, and they were recruiting. I asked them to tell me more about what they offered. In a nutshell, they said that since I was a veteran, I could sign up immediately as an advanced cadet. They would pay me $100, tax-free, every month, and in two years or less I would be commissioned as a second lieutenant in the US States Army. The good news was that I didn't have to go on active duty. I could go into the national guard or the inactive reserves. This sounded better and better, especially the money part. I also started thinking about what it would be like to hold a commission.

I immediately made my decision about which school I was going to attend and signed up on the spot. Of course the money didn't hurt, either. It may seem like a small amount today, but back then it was a lot.

Regardless of what factor I used to make my decision, I was going to be a soldier. At the time I had no intention of actually serving in the military again in any capacity. I endured a bad experience in the navy and was not interested in repeating it. I had thought about what it would be like to be an officer, though, and that part did interest me. I would get the commission, hang it on the wall, and make my mother proud of me. All I wanted to do as a profession was to be a police officer. I was having the time of my life and was sure that I had found my calling. I hung around the campus for a couple of months taking whatever subject interested me while waiting on classes to start at UTC.

The day soon came to start my quest as a true undergraduate. One of the first things I had to do was to get signed in at the ROTC department. Believe me, they were glad to see me. ROTC was not the most popular organization on college campuses at the time because the Vietnam War was still going on, and without the draft, few were interested. The ROTC department at UTC was on probation at the time I signed in and struggling to make its quota of enrollees. With my veteran status, I was just what they were looking for. I was issued all my uniforms and equipment and went to meet the commandant and staff. They said they were so glad to see me they were going to make me a cadet first sergeant. I had no clue what that was or where it fit into the rank structure. I didn't particularly care, either. I soon learned the rank wasn't bad for a first-year cadet.

I registered for a program called Human Services with Emphasis on Criminal Justice (CJ), which was a prelude to a full-fledged CJ program to be started a couple years later. As I had done before, I took every law course that I could find and continued with my plan of taking overloads whenever possible. I was really in "big school" now, and things were different. All the professors held doctoral degrees, and most were pure academicians. Some had really strange personalities and most didn't have enough common sense to get in out of the rain. But they held my career in the palms of their hands. One particular professor liked to role play. He would come into class dressed as a cowboy or railroad engineer, with all the getup and garb of the role. When he was in a role, he went all out with the lingo, characteristics, and mannerisms. I can't count all the different roles he played, but it was a lot. One day in class he just fell out. Passed out completely! An ambulance came and took him away, and we never saw him again. I think it was perhaps "role overload."

I had one slightly unnerving experience right after I began class at the UTC that had to do with a fellow student. About a year or so before, while I was attending junior college, I was on patrol one night when we received a call that an alarm was going off at a sporting goods store. Several of us rode the call, and when we arrived, we immediately saw that someone was inside the store. We yelled for them to get down on the floor and throw away any weapons. We didn't know how many were inside, and we didn't have a key to get in. The thieves had broken a large hole in the back wall of the store and went in that way. When we got there, two were in the process of carrying a large number of guns to the back in preparation for taking them out of the store. Two of us were directed to crawl inside, secure the two on the floor, and make sure no one else was inside. We crawled through the opening and got inside. We immediately handcuffed the two and then cleared the building. Once we were satisfied they were the only ones inside, we took them back through the hole and into the back of a patrol vehicle. Two people were arrested for the break-in and sent to prison.

I put the incident aside until I started at the university. One day I walked into class, and sitting in the front row was one of the guys we arrested for the break-in. We looked at each other, trying to recall from where we knew each other. After a few moments, it became apparent we both remembered. I was carrying my off-duty revolver and made sure that he saw it. We never spoke the entire semester, and I never saw him afterward. I never asked how he got out of prison or how he wound up at the university. I just watched my back from then on.

ROTC was coming along quite well with some exceptions. Every Wednesday was drill day, and we were expected to wear our uniforms on that day. I was still maintaining crazy hours at the police department (and still functioning with only a couple hours sleep) and wore my police uniform to class a lot. On Wednesdays, I had to bring my military uniform and change clothes on campus. We had military labs in the morning and drill that afternoon. Drill meant marching around, doing close order drills out on the parade field. This is where my former enlisted service paid off. I knew how to march and drill. Not much had changed since my basic training time, and it didn't take long to refresh my memory. Then one day it was time to take the PT test. A PT test is a physical fitness test designed to determine your physical capabilities. Back then, it involved pushups, sit-ups, a couple of really weird exercises, and a one-mile run. The test was held on the track of one of the local high schools, and we were to meet there early Saturday morning. It just so happened that I had to work the night before, so as always, I rushed from work to the track with no sleep. The bottom line is that I failed the first PT test I ever took. The navy wasn't big on physical fitness, so it never occurred to me to get into shape.

Well this was a wakeup call. I was going to have to start a regimen of exercises and running if I was going to make it in the army. I drove home that day dejected and hurt but determined that I was going to fix the problem. I started running every chance that I had and soon got my condition to where I never worried about a test again. I have taken many PT tests in the years since and have never failed.

Most weekends there was some sort of training planned. We were either going repelling, doing land navigation, or camping in some field for the weekend. The seniors usually played the role of opposing forces and provided some evaluation along the way. There is nothing crazier than twenty-five or so college students running around in the woods at night, firing blanks from an M16 rifle. It was a riot, and other than being exhausted from lack of sleep, it was actually fun.

One night stands out in my memory, though. We were doing some sort of night patrol. We were way out in the woods somewhere, trying to get back to the base camp. We came upon a creek and after checking our maps and compasses, realized we needed to be on the other side. We didn't know how deep the creek was but could see that it was flowing pretty fast. It was in the middle of the winter and cold as could be out there. We did some reconnaissance and found a tree across the creek that we thought we could use to cross. There was nothing to hold onto, and the tree was iced over, so the only way to cross on it was to sit down and scoot across. Several cadets made it across. Then it was my turn. I sat down on the log and started across, determined to make it. About halfway across the creek, my rifle started to shift on my back, and I tried to adjust it. This caused an imbalance, and I couldn't recover. Suddenly, I had a sinking feeling that I was slipping. There I went, off the log and into the rushing creek. The air temperature was probably twenty degrees or less, and the water was freezing cold. I gathered myself and made it to the other side, enduring the jeers of my fellow cadets.

There was nothing to do but stand the cold until we could find our way back. It seemed like hours until we finally made it, but what a welcome site that old camp building was. It had a big, old, coal-fired heater inside, and it was red hot. I got to my bunk, stripped, and climbed into bed. I hung all my clothes as close to the heater as I could to dry them out and could finally sense the feeling coming back into my feet and hands. Believe it or not, there was a teaching point in all this. Had we checked our maps carefully, we would not have been on the wrong side of the creek, and there would have been no need to risk drowning to get across.

Other weekends were spent on some firing range, learning marksmanship and weapon safety. Of course I had no trouble at all with this training, since I grew up around guns.

It was around this time that I met a man who would become a lifelong friend. Bill was a couple of years younger than I. We attended the same junior college, but I don't remember seeing him there. We started the ROTC program at the same time, and because we were both from Cleveland, we became close. Somehow I was ahead of Bill in class and senior to him in ROTC. Bill was into all sorts of karate stuff and was working on his black belt. One time he did a demonstration for the cadets. He brought in several big chunks of concrete. He lay down on the gym floor, placed the concrete on his chest, and had another cadet break the concrete with a sledgehammer. Needless to say, the other cadets were extremely impressed, and his stock as a cadet rose significantly.

Time came to start seriously preparing for summer camp. This is by far, the most important part of a cadet's training, and it is make or break. I started working out more and running a lot. I even signed up for a conditioning course at the university. It is the only course I ever dropped in my academic career. I signed up for it for one reason: to get in the best shape possible. I was not concerned about a grade or points. The course did exactly what I wanted. It was a gut-busting course that left me begging for air by day's end. But when it was over, I could hold my own on any road march or PT test.

There was only one more piece of business left before summer camp: the Military Ball, a formal event that is always held in the fanciest of facilities. The purpose is multifaceted. First, it recognizes the senior cadets and their dates. But more important, it gives cadets an opportunity to experience some of the pomp and circumstance that goes along with a career as a military officer. My wife and I went with Bill and his girlfriend, Joy.

I learned just before the ball that I was going to be recognized as a senior. This was due to maintaining my same attitude about overload. I basically was going to finish my degree in three years instead of the usual four.

We all were dressed to the nines, with Bill and I wearing formal military attire and our dates going all out with formal gowns. If you think this was all new to me, it was exceptionally new to my wife, who had never been to anything formal in her life. We made it through the night, and it wound up being one of the most memorable events of my life. I was starting to feel a little tingle about this officer and a gentleman thing. This wasn't bad!

Summer camp for us turned out to be in Kansas, and Bill and I decided to drive there in separate cars. It was at least a fifteen-hour drive, and we were going to try to make it nonstop. We loaded our vehicles with everything we could think of that might help us get through the next six weeks and pulled out. I had just purchased a new truck with a big V8 engine that drank gas like crazy. Maybe not such a great idea during the great gas shortage of the '70s. At times, gas was rationed in some places, and most stations closed early in the evening. People were shot waiting in line to get gas, and some situations turned into virtual riots. All over a tank of gas! Our trip was going great until we rolled into Paducah, Kentucky, at about 1:00 a.m., and every gas station in town was closed. My Chevy was wheezing on fumes, and we were going to be in big trouble if I didn't find some gas soon.

We drove around off the main road, hoping that some local store might be open and have some gas. No luck. I was about to give up when I spotted two police cars pulled up in a parking lot, and I decided I would drive over to them. I pulled up, showed them my badge, and explained our dilemma. One said to the other, "Call old Jim that runs the Quick Mart. He can come in and get this guy some gas." The other guy got on the radio and called his dispatch, telling them to call Jim and tell him to get down there pronto. They told us to follow them to the station, and after a few minutes, Jim pulled up. He was none too happy about being awakened at that hour, but he pumped me a tank of gas anyway. We paid Jim, thanked the two officers, and drove on our way to Kansas. I have never used a badge to get into or out of anything, but that was an exception. The "brotherhood" worked that night, and I was certainly glad.

We finally made it to the Fort and started the processing. We parked our vehicles and boarded a bus that took us to our respective company areas. Bill and I were assigned to separate companies and only saw each other a couple of times during the six-week camp.

My life changed dramatically as soon as I stepped off the bus. Since I was a veteran and a little older than most of the cadets, the cadre was waiting as I stepped off. Somehow my veteran status automatically made me a leader of men. I was immediately put in charge of the platoon, given a mouthful of instructions, and told to get them off the parade ground. Fortunately for me, I had been warned that this may happen by the cadre back at the university, so I was prepared. I knew what to do, where to go, and how to get there. I could bark orders with the best of them. Another good thing in my favor was that the majority of the cadets were young and stupid. Most of them didn't know their left foot from their right and didn't know whether I did, either. I must have impressed somebody because after the first day, I never had one moment of trouble with the camp cadre.

I had other opportunities to demonstrate my leadership ability and never had a problem. I am sure that the first day set the stage for the rest of camp. My summer camp was the last all-male camp ever, as the next year, females started attending as well. But that year, it was just a bunch of guys from all over the country. Different schools and different attitudes, but we were all there for the same reason.

Summer camp was busy and never stopped for the entire six weeks. I did things at camp that even today scare the heck out of me. But at the time, there was no time to be scared. The most frightening for me were the water drills. There were a couple of exercises that involved really high places out over water. One in particular was called the slide for life. In this exercise, we climbed up a two-hundred-foot tower to a platform at the top. Once we reached the top, we were told to sit down and grab a tee bar that was attached to a long cable running down to the water below. We did a half chin-up, and away we went for what seemed like forever. Down below, a flagman signaled us when to let go, and we slammed into the water, hopefully feet first. Another exercise involved low crawling out onto a two-inch rope that was stretched between two poles in the water. The rope was forty-five feet from the water, and we had to crawl out to the center and hang by our hands over the water. We then had to tell the cadre our name and school and ask for permission to drop. The cadre gave us some additional instructions, such as to look up, and then told us to drop. I hit the water and kicked to the surface.

The problem with both exercises was that the equipment was just thrown together. The tower swayed back and forth as we climbed, and there was no safety hook or net. If we fell, it was on us. A couple of guys refused to do one of the exercises, and after considerable coaxing, were sent home. I don't like high places and don't particularly like water, but I was not about to leave under those circumstances. I hung in and completed everything I was asked to do.

Over the course of the camp, we fired every weapon in the army's arsenal at the time. We had hands-on instruction, including throwing hand grenades. This was another scary time I would not like to do ever again. We had to get down into a pit with an instructor, and it was barely big enough for the two of us to stand. After a period of intense instruction, we were given a live hand grenade and told to toss it at a target in front of us. Simple, right? Well it is if you don't drop the grenade after you pull the pin. If that happens, you are in big trouble because of the close quarters. If neither you nor the instructor can recover the grenade in a really short amount of time, you are probably both going to be killed or seriously injured. Of course, I followed the instructions to the letter and breathed a big sigh of relief the moment the grenade left my hand, headed in the direction of the target. I don't know if they pay those instructors hazardous duty pay, but they should. Tossing that live grenade is undoubtedly one of the most dangerous things I have ever done.

One of the many awards one can earn at summer camp is the Recondo badge. The cadre used to call it the coveted Recondo badge and really sold us on its importance in our careers. The truth is, if you told anyone after you were on active duty that you held the coveted Recondo badge, they would laugh you out of the Officers Club, but at the time, it was a pretty big deal. I set my sights on the badge from the beginning and was closing in on it. I scored well on the PT test and had completed all the other requirements except land navigation.

Land navigation is basically going from point A to point B using a map and compass. I had to set up the map properly, estimate how far I was from a particular landmark, and head in that direction. I had to have some method of judging how far I had gone. Most use a pace method; you measure your own pace and then count how many steps you have taken. This will give you a rough guess as to how close you are to your target. To pass this test you had to find a certain number of hidden targets within an allotted time frame. Each of the targets counted a certain number of points, and you needed so many points to pass.

Now all I needed to do was pass the land navigation course, and I would be Recondo qualified. Within a half hour or so after starting the course, I had accumulated enough points to pass and could have quit right then. But no! I had to destroy this course. I had to show everyone how good I was at land navigation, so I kept on going. I wanted to amass as many points as I could. Suddenly, I looked around and was hopelessly lost. Kansas is rather flat and has very few distinguishable landmarks. I was completely flustered. I didn't know my left from right, and time was running out. I stumbled around for a couple of hours, until I finally found my way back to the finish point. By this time, I had used up all the points I had accumulated and lost any chance of the Recondo. I had no one to blame but myself and could only rack this up as another teaching point.

About midway through summer camp, we were told that we were going to be off for the Fourth of July holiday and could actually leave the base. Bill and I got together and decided to drive over to Lawrence, where his grandparents lived, and spend the weekend there. We loaded up in his little Triumph and took off. For three days we lived like normal people. We slept in a normal bed, ate normal food, and could actually have a beer. It was a great break from camp, and his folks could not have been nicer. They really rolled out the red carpet for us and made me feel like part of the family. Much too soon it was time to head back to the base and finish the next two weeks.

Just as soon as we got back to camp, I learned that I would be going home a week early. It seems that if you were set to graduate in December, you could cut the camp short by one week to ensure you were there to start classes on time. Whatever the reason, I was ecstatic. Summer camp was okay, but there was nothing like going home. I started getting ready and packing everything I could in order to get a head start. I finished up the last week and started the out processing.

In the meantime, the platoon had an opportunity to go to a picnic on a lake. I don't remember why we got to go, but it was another nice break. While we were there, some of my fellow platoon members decided that since I was getting to leave early, they should give me a going-away present. They surrounded me, snatched me up, and threw me into the lake, clothes and all. It was all in good fun. And considering all the beer we had consumed, it was no big deal.

I finished the out processing, and on the last day there, the platoon went on about the business of training. I had said my good-byes that morning, and all I had to do was finish loading and be on my way. Another member of the platoon was also leaving, and he asked if I would give him a ride to the airport on my way. Well I couldn't refuse, so he loaded up as well. I dropped him off at the small airport near the base. As he was leaving, he asked to borrow $20. I gave him the money, and he said he would send it back to me as soon as possible. I never heard from him again and never got the money back. I guess not everybody who goes through summer camp is necessarily a gentleman.

I headed east across Kansas and into Missouri, determined to drive straight through. I admit that I kept the hammer down the entire trip, going much faster than I should have. I actually broke the speedometer on the truck going home. Along the way, I picked up a hitchhiker somewhere in Missouri. He was a young, black guy going to Jacksonville, Florida, and he rode with me all the way to Chattanooga. It was good to have some company, and I certainly remembered what it was like to try catching a ride somewhere. He went to sleep somewhere along the way, and when he woke up, I was flying. He looked out and saw the telephone poles flashing by and almost fainted. He looked over at the speedometer and I am sure didn't believe his eyes. We made it to Chattanooga in one piece, and I said good-bye to him. Only twenty-five miles to go, and I would be home.

By the time that I got there, I was totally exhausted. I barely had the energy to take a shower and make it to bed. To this day, I remember taking that shower and what a feeling it was to be in my own house in a private shower. One of the nice souvenirs that I had from summer camp was a ring of chiggers around my waist and both ankles. Kansas must be the national chigger capital of the world, and a lot of them came home with me. It would be days before I got that cleared up.

My son was asleep when I got there, so it was about twelve hours before I saw him. I had been able to call home just a couple of times while I was away, and the last time, I asked him what he wanted me to bring him when I came home. He wanted a Mickey Mouse watch. I bought him one at the post exchange and couldn't wait to give it to him.

After a couple of days of "R and R," it was back to business and classes. I had one more semester to go, and graduation would be mine. I started thinking about what I was going to do after graduation. I could stay as a small-town police officer, but that really wasn't going anywhere. I was having fun, but that was about the only benefit to the job. I considered going to a federal agency or maybe some state agency, but nothing really reached out to me.

As luck would have it, something happened that made the decision for me. When the federal budget was released that year, the military got one of the largest pay increases in history. Salaries went up 14 percent. This got my attention, and I started looking at pay scales for the military. I soon learned that with my prior years of service, I would triple my salary and have some of the best benefits available anywhere. Since I was about to be a college graduate, it was not hard to figure out what the best thing to do was. I immediately went to the ROTC administration and applied for active duty. Since I was a veteran, I had a choice, and I was taking it. I was accepted, and now all I had to do was choose a branch of the army in which I wanted to serve. For me, there was only one branch, and that was the military police.

In about two weeks, I received my branch assignment orders to—gasp—the quartermaster corps! What did those guys even do? I have since learned that they are storekeepers, oilmen, and supply clerks, none of which appealed to me at the time.

I immediately filed an appeal and got everyone I knew to write letters. When I asked the branch assignment office why I had been assigned to that branch, I was asked what qualifications I had for the military police corps. I replied, "What qualifications do you think I have to be in the quartermaster corps?" Fortunately, in a few weeks, I had it straightened out and was assigned to the military police branch, after all.

The only thing left to do now was finish some papers, pass a couple of tests, and graduate. Unfortunately, I had two extensive papers to finish and only a short time to get them done. I hit the books and burned the midnight oil to make it happen. One of the papers that I wrote was a thesis titled "The Psychology of Speaking in Tongues." I got interested in this subject during my Holiness Church days. I had always been interested in what possessed those people to babble that way. What was the motivation? What was the purpose? Were they actually receiving some sort of divine intervention? I set out to answer all these questions and more. I spent several days writing the paper, and when I went to turn in everything for graduation, I had twenty-five books checked out of the library.

The next month was a flurry of activity, getting uniforms bought and getting ready for the great adventure ahead. I would be commissioned in December but would not actually graduate until the following May because there was no winter graduation. It was simply a matter of semantics as far as I was concerned. The most important thing was the commissioning.

The speaker for the ceremony went on and on. As I heard him start to wrap up, I began to come back to reality. In just a few short moments, it would be over. The commandant of the ROTC department thanked the speaker for his kind remarks and then turned his attention to us. "Cadets will please rise! Raise your right hand and repeat after me: 'I, David L. Lyons, having been appointed a second lieutenant in the United States Army, do solemnly swear or affirm that I will support and defend the Constitution of the United States against all enemies, foreign and domestic; that I will bear true faith and allegiance to the same; that I take this obligation freely, without any mental reservation or purpose of evasion; and that I will well and faithfully discharge the office upon which I am about to enter. So help me God.'"

The commandant's next words were, "You may pin your officers." With that, my wife and my mother pinned on the shiny gold bars my uncle gave me. They are the same ones used when he received a field commission during the Korean War, and they made the ceremony even more special. After receiving a congratulatory kiss from my wife, I stood by to receive congratulations from the cadets who were assembled, as well as the cadre and staff. And just like that, it was over. My life was changed forever that day in more ways than I could ever imagine.

I had just beaten the odds and made it out of Alabama for good. After a short stay at the reception, I rounded up my little boy, and we made our way to the door. As I walked out of the center, there stood Master Sergeant Boatwright. As I got closer, he snapped me a crisp military salute. As his right hand touched his temple I heard, "Congratulations, Sir!" as his other hand was held open, waiting for the customary payment for the salute. I returned his salute and reached into my pocket. As I placed the silver dollar into his left hand, I said, "Thank you for everything, Master Sergeant. I could not have made it without your help." This man, this sergeant, who yelled at me, pushed me, and molded me, had just afforded me the greatest symbol of respect that a subordinate soldier can offer. As I walked away, I knew in my heart that I had received far more from him than a salute. I paused just outside the building, taking a few moments to let the events of the day soak in.

All of those reflections I had conjured up during the speech came flooding back. And as I stood there, one overriding thought kept entering my mind. I am, indeed, a long way from Whitehall.

CHAPTER 24

Recipes, Potions, and Such

I decided to include several recipes for some of the foods I grew up eating. These are simple foods, and the recipes are as best as I can remember them. I also decided to include some of the more important home remedies I remember my grandmother using. Please do not think that I am practicing medicine without a license. Nor am I encouraging anyone to try them. They are included here simply for your reading enjoyment.

Nanny's Made from Scratch Cornbread

For many years, my grandfather took corn we grew to the grist mill for grinding into cornmeal. He hauled a wagonload of corn to the mill and returned with a few sacks of ground meal. The cornmeal contained most of the corn husk and required sifting prior to using. This recipe predated store-bought self-rising and required the addition of baking powder to get the cornbread to rise.

Ingredients

1 cup of cornmeal, sifted
½ cup of flour, sifted
2 teaspoons baking powder
¾ cup buttermilk
½ teaspoon baking soda
1 egg
1 tablespoon lard

Mix the dry ingredients in bowl. Add buttermilk and egg, mix until even consistency. Grease a cast iron skillet with lard and pour in mixture. Place into hot oven, and bake thirty minutes.

Hoe Cakes (sometimes called corn fritters)

This was an absolute favorite of mine as a child, and I think it was because I could hold the cake in my hands easily. There are probably other reasons, but that will do for now. Hoe cakes were quick and made good use of the hot surface of the wood stove when everything else was done.

Ingredients:
Nanny's made from Scratch Cornbread mix
lard

Coat the hot stove surface with an adequate amount of lard, being careful not to set the house on fire from the hot lard.
Spoon the cornbread mixture onto the stove, keeping the cakes about four to six inches in diameter.
Allow to brown, and turn. Brown second side.

Red Eye Gravy

This traditional Southern dish was enjoyed during those few months when sugar-cured ham was available. This didn't occur often, but when it did, we made the most of it.

Ingredients
large slice of sugar-cured ham
coffee

Place ham into heated cast iron skillet.
Allow to sizzle, about five to ten minutes.
Remove ham to a plate.
Pour one cup black coffee over the ham.
Serve with Nanny's Cathead biscuits.

Homestyle "Cathead" Biscuits

For all the years that I was around my grandfather, he called Nanny's biscuits Catheads. I never knew why, other than perhaps they somehow looked like a cat's head. Many mornings he crumbled one of her biscuits into a saucer and poured his heavily-sugared coffee over it.

Ingredients
3 cups flour, sifted
1 teaspoon salt
1 tablespoon baking powder
½ teaspoon baking soda
3 tablespoons lard
1 cup buttermilk

Nanny always made her biscuits right in the flour bin. She mixed the buttermilk and lard in with the flour until firm and then added the other ingredients. The most important step in making biscuits is properly kneading the mixture. She took the mixture out of the bin, put it on her dough board, and kneaded until the consistency suited her. She then floured the dough board and rolled out the mixture with her special rolling pin (which was a Miller High Life beer bottle). She rolled the mixture until it was about one-half to one-inch thick. Then she cut out the biscuits with her cutter, a spotlessly clean, empty Vienna sausage can. I suppose they came out just the right size for her, so that's what she used. She placed the biscuits into a greased cast iron skillet and baked in a hot oven for ten to fifteen minutes.

Sweet Potato Biscuits

This delicious twist on Nanny's biscuits was, unfortunately, seasonal and only came around during harvest. Sweet potatoes have a fairly short shelf life, so when they came in, we had to find innovative ways to cook them. This was one of the best.

Ingredients
Homestyle Cathead Biscuit mix
Several sweet potatoes, peeled and cut into chunks
1 cup water
3 teaspoons brown sugar
¼ teaspoon cinnamon
⅛ teaspoon allspice
5 tablespoons butter

Place sweet potatoes into saucepan with water. Bring to boil.
Cook sweet potatoes until easily mashed with a fork or masher.
Add butter and the dry ingredients.
Stir constantly, until all ingredients have blended.
Pour mixture onto dough board and knead into biscuit mix.
Cut with Vienna sausage can (or biscuit cutter) and place into heated and greased skillet.
Serve hot with butter.

Sausage Gravy and Biscuits

Biscuits and gravy were a staple at our house. I think the main reason was its simplicity and the fact we had biscuits every morning. I don't think that my grandfather could have lived if he didn't start the day with catheads. Most of the time, however, we didn't have sausage to add to the mixture, which was just fine with us. Gravy without sausage is commonly called sawmill gravy. Fancy places sometimes refer to it as white sauce.

Ingredients
3 cups of milk
5–6 tablespoons sifted flour
Salt and pepper to taste
6 ounces (more or less) of sausage or bacon
2 tablespoons lard

Put sausage or bacon into cast iron skillet. If sausage or bacon is not fully cooked, allow time to do so.
Add lard and allow to bubble.
Add flour and whisk, blending mixture together.
Add milk.
Stir constantly until gravy thickens.
Remove from heat and serve.

If you are making sawmill gravy, simply leave out the sausage or bacon. Heat lard and add flour. When ingredients are thoroughly mixed, add milk, and stir until gravy thickens.
Halve biscuits and pour gravy mixture over them.

Fried Apple or Peach Pies

We cooked on an old-fashioned woodstove, which took a long time to get hot. When it finally reached optimum temperature, Nanny didn't waste it. She had the oven full of something, water boiling for dishes, flat irons heating, and every inch of stove surface full of something. She often made hoecakes right on the stove, but every now and then, when fruit was available, she made fried pies. The fancy name for these would be "turnovers," but the name didn't matter. They were good no matter what they were called.

Ingredients
Dough
4 cups sifted flour
2 teaspoons salt
1 cup lard
1 cup buttermilk

Filling
6–8 peeled apples or peaches, cut into chunks
¾ cup sugar
water to cover
2 tablespoons. lard

Mix flour and salt in a large mixing bowl.
Add lard and mix until mixture becomes crumbly.
Add milk and knead into a ball.
Roll out dough onto a floured dough board and in approximately six-inch circles. Set aside until filling is ready.

Place fruit into saucepan, and add sugar and water to cover.
Cover pan, and cook over low heat until fruit falls apart.
Remove lid, and cook until water evaporates.
Grease stove surface with lard and heat.
Spoon filling onto dough, and fold over. Seal dough with the tines of a fork dipped in water.
Place pies onto greased stove surface. Cook until the underside is brown, and then turn. Brown the other side.
Note: Powder or regular sugar can be added to the pie once it has been removed from heat and allowed to cool.

Souse Meat (Hogshead Cheese)

Nanny didn't waste anything, especially when it came to food. We usually had a hog that we fattened up all year and slaughtered in the late fall. For a short while, meat was plentiful, and life was good. Unfortunately, we didn't have any kind of refrigeration, and keeping meat was a challenge. Much of a hog can be kept for long periods by either smoking or curing with salt. The rest has to be eaten as soon as possible after butchering. Sausage and bacon cuts were kept as long as possible, and the rest was turned into somewhat of a delicacy called souse meat. Some folks refer to this as hogshead cheese (or headcheese), but it was always souse to us. Souse uses all the parts of the hog that are not suitable to be cooked alone, such as the head, tongue, feet, and ears. Some folks eat pig's feet, and some chow down on pig's ears, but not Nanny. For her to eat those parts, it had to be in souse meat. Suffice to say, souse meat was an acquired taste. However, when you are hungry enough, what you are eating doesn't really matter.

Ingredients
Any cuts of hog meat not used for sausage, bacon, or curing. The head is the main source for souse meat.
salt and pepper to taste
1 cup vinegar
hot red peppers, finely chopped
sage to taste
onion, finely chopped

Boil the head, ears, feet, tongue, and so on until fork tender.
Remove meat and mash into a paste.
Mix in the remaining ingredients and place in a shallow pan.
Place in a cool place overnight or until jelled.

Fried Chicken

We always had chickens running around in the yard. There was a chicken coop in back of the house, where the chickens roost at night. Most of the time, Nanny would let a "settin'" hen sit on a batch of eggs until they hatched and then take the babies inside until they were old enough to survive the wild animals looking for a meal. The baby chicks were called biddies and were great fun for a small boy to watch run around in the box they were in. The hens were kept for laying, and the roosters were culled to become Sunday dinner. Nanny would not have too many roosters around because they fought. Besides, why feed something that doesn't produce anything in return?

We didn't have fried chicken every Sunday. Most of the time this dinner was reserved for when someone came to visit, like the cousins. However, when we did fry chicken, it was an adventure. Nanny went into the yard and selected the hapless rooster that would have the honor of feeding us. I think the selection process was whichever one she could catch. Sometimes, she got me to help her catch the bird. As soon as she had the bird in hand, she grabbed it by the neck and swung it wildly around and around, until the head came apart from the rest. The body of the rooster went flying through the air and flopped around until all the life was gone from the poor bird.

Once the bird was completely dead, she picked it up and started the plucking process. This involved removing all the feathers from the bird by hand. Once the feathers were removed, she cut open the bird and removed the entrails, being careful to keep the edible parts separate for later. She then held the bird over an open flame to singe away all the tiny pin feathers and skin follicles.

When she was satisfied that the bird was clean, she cut it up for frying. Every part of the bird was used for something. If a part couldn't be breaded and fried, she saved it for dressing or giblet gravy.

Ingredients

1 rooster plucked, singed, and cut up	flour
enough lard to fill the cast iron skillet	salt and pepper to taste

Mix flour, salt, and pepper thoroughly.
Fill skillet with lard, and bring to soft boil.
Place chicken parts into the flour mixture, making sure the entire surface is covered by the flour mixture.
Place the chicken parts into the hot lard. Cook thoroughly, turning as necessary.

Cornbread Sage Dressing

This is one of my favorite foods ever. The only time we got to eat this dish was when company came, and Nanny cooked fried chicken.

Ingredients
cornbread
1 medium onion
6 celery stalks
1 cup cooked chicken meat
2 cups chicken broth
sage to taste
salt and pepper to taste

Preheat oven to 350 degrees.
Crumble cornbread into large mixing bowl.
Cut chicken into tiny pieces; add to cornbread.
Dice celery and onion.
Pour chicken broth into a saucepan and add celery and onion. Cook over medium heat until celery and onion soften.
Pour chicken broth mix into the cornbread and stir until thoroughly wet.
Add sage, salt, and pepper to taste.
Place in greased baking dish and bake at 350 degrees until brown..

Fried Squirrel

Now this is a dish that I never got used to. Even though meat was scarce and anything beat going hungry, I just couldn't get into squirrel. I did, however, shoot more than my share of the critters, and being from a family that didn't believe in wasting anything, I brought them home to Nanny. She was more than willing to fry them up, and my grandfather actually liked the dish.

Nanny first skinned the animal and removed the entrails. She put the squirrel it in a bowl of salt brine overnight. This was supposed to remove the gamey taste. The next day she cut the squirrel into four pieces, dipped them in breading, and fried in hot grease.

Ingredients
1 squirrel, skinned with entrails removed
enough lard to fill a cast iron skillet
sifted flour
salt and pepper to taste

Cut squirrel into four pieces.
Dip into flour, salt, and pepper mixture.
Drop into hot lard. Turn as needed.

Fried Rabbit

See above, and substitute rabbit for squirrel.

Combo Plate

See above, and combine squirrel and rabbit.

Nanner Pudding

We rarely had this Southern delicacy, but when we did, it was a memorable occasion. Bananas were hard to come by and even harder to keep fresh for any length of time. Nanny usually made this dish when company came.

Ingredients
1½ cups sugar
2 cups milk
½ cup sifted flour
2 tablespoons cornstarch
4 eggs
1 package of Nilla wafers
2 teaspoons vanilla extract
8–10 bananas

Combine all dry ingredients in a mixing bowl.
Pour milk into a saucepan, and bring to boil.
Separate the egg yolks and slowly pour into hot milk, stirring constantly.
Add dry ingredients, stirring constantly to break up any clumps.
As soon as mixture begins to thicken, add vanilla extract and remove from heat.
Slice bananas, and line a shallow baking dish with alternating layers of bananas and wafers. Carefully pour the liquid mixture over the bananas and wafers.
Allow to cool.

If you desire a meringue over the pie, simply take the egg whites and beat until fluffy.
Spoon the finished meringue over the pie, and bake at 350 degrees for approximately five minutes, or until brown.

Peanut Brittle

We grew peanuts for most of my early childhood. They were one of those things that we seemed to take for granted growing up. Every year they were there, and we never gave them much thought. Nanny made several delicious treats from the peanuts, but the best was peanut brittle. Unfortunately for me, she usually made batches of the stuff to send to one or more of the men in the family who were off serving in the military. I realize now what a sacrifice they were making, but at the time, it just didn't seem fair that they got all the brittle.

Ingredients
2 cups raw peanuts
2 cups granulated sugar
1 cup corn syrup (Nanny used sorghum syrup because that's what we had)
1 tablespoon baking soda
½ cup water
1 teaspoon vanilla extract
⅛ teaspoon salt
1 tablespoon butter

Bring water, corn syrup, sugar, salt, and peanuts to boil. Stir constantly. Cover for one minute and then remove lid. Cook until mixture starts to thicken.
Remove from heat, and add baking soda, vanilla extract, and butter. Stir for approximately thirty seconds.
Pour onto greased cookie sheets. The baking soda will cause the mixture to expand quickly, so it is important to pour onto the sheet quickly.
Allow to cool and then break into pieces.

Beans and Taters

We never fixed this staple at home, but I ate my weight of it at other people's houses. I have no idea why Nanny didn't fix it, but she never did. I knew people who had beans and potatoes for every meal.

Ingredients

1 pound dry pinto beans	10 potatoes, peeled and cut into quarters
water to cover	water to cover
¼ pound fatback	

Wash and carefully check beans for small rocks.
Place in pan over medium heat, cover with water, and fatback for seasoning.
Wash potatoes and place in pan. Add fatback, cover with water, and boil over medium heat until mushy.
Serve beans with potatoes. Cornbread really makes this dish, along with some chow chow or relish.

Turnip Greens

We ate a lot of turnip greens and turnips. Nanny always planted a row or two of the prolific vegetable, and when they came in, we had to eat them quickly as there was no way of keeping them once they were picked. Most Southern families at that time ate collard greens, but for some reason, Nanny would not allow them in her house. So turnips it was.

Ingredients

turnip greens with turnip removed	turnips
water to cover	fatback

Wash greens thoroughly, and remove stems.
Place in saucepan, add turnips and fatback, and cover with water.
Cook until tender.

Sauerkraut

The only two reasons I can think of for Nanny making this dish is that cabbage was abundant and easy to grow, and that my granddaddy liked it. She always planted several rows of cabbage, and when it came in, she used some for homemade soup, some she canned, and the rest was made into sauerkraut. She made hers in a big, glazed, crock churn she used only for kraut. The churn has survived, and I have it today.

Ingredients
10–15 heads of cabbage, washed thoroughly, cored and cut into wedges (The amount of cabbage will depend on the container size that you intend to use.)
pickling or canning salt (Iodized salt will not work.)

Shred the cabbage into thin strips using a sharp knife or kraut knife
Add three tablespoons of salt for every five pounds of cabbage. Distribute salt evenly to ensure the cabbage is thoroughly covered.
Let sit for ten minutes. The cabbage will begin to wilt as the salt will draw the juices from the cabbage.
Pack the mixture firmly into selected container. You must use a glass jar or crock. Do not use metal or wood.
Tamp mixture periodically to squeeze the juice until the cabbage is completely covered.
Cover mixture airtight. Air prohibits the fermentation process and can lead to molding.
Place container in a well-ventilated location with a relatively constant temperature (68–72 degrees).
Keep for three to four weeks. Check mixture daily for mold on surface. If mold appears, scrape off and discard.
Remove mixture from crock, and store in a cool place. (Nanny would can the kraut as soon as she removed it from her crock.)

Poke Salad

The poke bush grows wild in most parts of the South. The bush grows from six to eight feet in height and can be as big as three to four inches in diameter at the base. During the fall, bright red berries grow on the bush, much like grapes. Back in the day, the juice from poke berries was used for many things, from dying clothes to putting war paint on Indian horses. It has been said that the original Constitution of the United States was written with ink made from the juice of poke berries.

The poke bush is extremely poisonous, yet it remains one of the most eaten wild vegetables ever. Nanny cooked poke salad throughout my childhood, and I never got sick. Nor do I remember anyone in the family being sick from eating poke salad. Either she knew how to fix it right, or we were extremely lucky. I do know that she was very careful when she picked the leaves from the poke bush, and she always said that if they weren't exactly right, you could die from eating them. She picked only the very young and tender shoots from low on the bush. There could be no color in the leaves whatsoever. She took the leaves home and rinsed them several times before putting them on to cook.

Poke salad looks a lot like spinach when cooked down, but has a strong, odd taste that takes some getting used to. However, when you are hungry and that's all there is, it tastes pretty good.

Ingredients
poke salad leaves (young, tender, and from low on the bush)
water to cover
fatback

Wash leaves carefully, rinsing several times.
Place in saucepan, add fatback, and cover with water.
Cook over medium heat until leaves are tender.
Serve with fresh green onions and cornbread.

Sassafras Tea

This is a Southern drink enjoyed by millions for years. The sassafras bush grows wild in the Southern states. Its roots are dug up and removed from the rest of the bush. They are then cleaned and boiled. The more tender roots farther away from the main bush are the best. The root of the bush contains an oil called safrole. At one time, it was considered medicinal for both humans and animals. The oil from the sassafras bush was once used as the main ingredient for root beer. However, today it is believed that safrole can cause cancer and is banned by the Food and Drug Administration. Once again, a childhood treasure has been deemed to be harmful if consumed. It sure was good while it lasted, though, as Nanny made several big pots of tea each fall. As with many other foods that we ate, we never got sick, not even a little bit.

Ingredients
sassafras roots
water
sugar

Dig roots, and remove from main bush. Scrape clean, and rinse several times to make sure all dirt is removed.
Place in large pot of water and bring to a boil.
Remove from heat and add sugar.
Let cool and enjoy.

Hominy

Hominy is made from corn, and we grew a lot of corn on our farm. Corn had many uses, from providing feed for our animals, being ground into cornmeal, or cooked by one of several different means. Growing up, one of my favorite corn recipes was hominy. Hominy is basically puffed corn with the husks removed. The Southern delicacy grits is made by grinding hominy. It may be hard to believe, but we never ate grits. I don't know if it was because my grandfather didn't like them or if it was Nanny. But whatever the reason, we never had them. In fact, I had never heard of grits until I went into the military.

The secret to hominy is to remove the tough outer skin or husk. This is done by soaking the corn in an alkaline solution until the skin is softened and falls away. Nanny used lye for this purpose, but you can use baking soda as well. Back in the day, some folks made their own lye from ashes and mixed it with water to soak the corn in. I never remember Nanny doing that, and she always had a can of Red Devil Lye handy.

Ingredients
4 cups of corn kernels (yellow or white)
4 teaspoons lye
water to cover for soaking
water to cover for cooking
fatback

Mix lye and water together and allow to thoroughly dissolve.
Add corn and let soak for eight to twelve hours.
Rinse thoroughly, and remove puffed corn from mixture, separating it from the husks.
Place the corn in a saucepan. Add fatback and cover with water.
Cook over medium heat until tender.
Serve with butter.

Home Remedies

As I mentioned earlier, we rarely went to a doctor. When we did, it was usually a serious matter. Nanny had all sorts of mountain remedies for most every ailment. She knew all about herbs and potions for humans, as well as for animals. She kept the cow in good health, along with all of us. I wish that I had paid more attention to what she did. What would have really been special would be to have had a camcorder or movie camera to video her talking about the various cures she used. But I didn't pay attention and, of course, didn't have any means back then of recording her. So all I have are memories. I can only recall a few of her remedies, and they may not be exact. I am only mentioning them for discussion purposes. None of these remedies should be experimented with or tried at home.

Potato Poultice

Nanny used a poultice for all sorts of problems. I have no idea how it worked, but it did. Some of the more common reasons for its application were boils, sties, and embedded splinters.

To make a poultice, take a fresh Irish potato, and cut it in half. Use a spoon to scrape out the meat of the potato onto a clean piece of cloth. Cheesecloth is best, but if you don't have that, any clean cloth, or even a paper coffee filter, will work. Make sure that the juice of the potato can seep through the cloth. Apply to the affected area. Secure with a bandage or tape, and let set overnight.

Mountain Cough Syrup

If this remedy doesn't cure your cold or cough, it will certainly make you forget you have it. Nanny always had a pint or two of this close by, especially in the wintertime. The longer it set the better it worked, so she kept it going all the time.

To make it, you need a pint of moonshine whiskey and several sticks of peppermint candy. Place the peppermint in the jar of whiskey and cover. Let sit until needed. Use sparingly.

Really Awful Tasting Cough Medicine

I can still remember having to take this stuff because once you do, it is ingrained into your brain forever. Nanny would take a spoonful of powdered sulfur and pour several drops of coal oil in it. The sulfur was bad enough, and the coal oil only made it worse.

Vinegar and Brown Paper Splint

I know for a fact that this works because I saw Nanny set my brother's broken arm and wrap it in a cast made from brown paper soaked in cider vinegar. Within a day or two, the arm was healed completely.

Soak brown paper from a grocery bag in brown cider vinegar, and wrap the affected area. Secure with twine and place into a sling if possible. After two days, remove and rewrap as needed.

Mullein

Mullein is a plant that grew wild in the woods and fields of our farm. It grows close to the ground and has fuzzy leaves. Nanny used the plant for various remedies for both human and animal ailments. For us, she boiled the leaves into a tea for cold treatment, upset stomach, and other maladies. The oil can be extracted from the plant and used for all sorts of muscular aches and pains, as well as for the treatment of hemorrhoids. She chopped the leaves into small pieces and fed them to our milk cow, along with her regular feed. I never knew what she was treating but whatever it was, the mullein seemed to work.

Baking Soda and Vinegar

I remember my grandfather using this remedy often for upset stomach or indigestion. He poured apple cider vinegar into a cup and added one teaspoon of baking soda.

Caution! When baking soda is introduced to vinegar, a fairly violent chemical reaction occurs, and the mixture foams up considerably.

Coal Oil

The term "coal oil" was used throughout my childhood. The reality is that what they were really using was pure kerosene. I won't go into the chemical differences because the two terms have been used interchangeably for years. Nanny used kerosene primarily in our lamps for lighting. However, she used the product for medicinal purposes, as well. I related the story earlier about jumping off the foot log and sticking a nail through my foot. When I got home, Nanny promptly put my foot into a pan full of kerosene. Kerosene apparently has some serious disinfectant qualities and may even speed up the healing process. Nanny used kerosene for a variety of medicinal purposes, not the least of which was for the treatment of colds and coughs.

Sugar Tit

This decidedly sexist term was used to describe the world's earliest pacifier. Babies became cranky long before the invention of the "binky," and folks came up with all sorts of innovative ways to quiet the fussy child. Nanny's solution was to put about a teaspoon of sugar into a piece of cloth and tie it off, forming somewhat of a nipple. The baby sucked on the cloth and enjoyed the sugar high it produced.

Paregoric

Paregoric was one of very few store-bought remedies that we used. The main ingredient in paregoric is powdered opium, and this caused it to be highly regulated by the early 1960s. Prior to the government getting involved, its use was widespread. It was a household necessity, especially if small children were involved. Anytime one of us suffered from an earache or toothache, the best course of action was a teaspoon of paregoric. The narcotic effect calmed even the most painful problems and allowed the rest of the household to get a good night's sleep.

CPSIA information can be obtained
at www.ICGtesting.com
Printed in the USA
LVHW010355150520
655594LV00001B/2/J